Advance Pr

Life is predictably unpredictable a.... ..../ ... ...
couragement and disillusionment... especially towards God. Let Dwyer
shape your emerging, messy journey through careful observation of hers,
rediscovering hope in the most unlikely of places—not towards religion,
but to the person of Jesus.

—Douglas A. Balzer
Church effectiveness coach
Author of *The Empowerment Pivot* and *Light Up the Dark*

Michelle Dwyer has written a timely and absolutely necessary book on
spiritual healing. Each chapter brings up another area of healing that
needs to happen in most human souls and her chapters always involve a
very relatable story. Although the concepts presented are deep and theologically true, the writing is entirely approachable and reader-friendly. I
highly recommend *Fierce Hope*.

—Chet Kennedy
Youth worker and author of *Broken Mortals*

If anyone has any doubt about whether Michelle Dwyer lives what she's
sharing in this book, I am here to speak to your doubt. I have walked
closely with Michelle personally and in ministry. She has rumbled with,
wrestled through, and ultimately lived out every principle, tool, and topic
she discusses in this book. You are getting the real deal; she has amazingly
succeeded in communicating and imparting her compassion, fierceness,
wisdom, and undying hope in this book. Take it from me, from someone
who was formerly apathetic and hopeless and now is filled with hope and
vibrancy: these concepts and principles create space for Jesus to bring life,
freedom, and hope. I know that is what Jesus has done for me and He can
do it for you as you journey through this book. Let hope arise!

—Amy Cheetham
Pastor and podcast co-host

Fierce Hope reminded me that hope is not complacent, but a steady, driving force that takes us to our God-given best. Michelle shares parts of her journey and draws you along, making it easy to walk through healing steps. I am better for having experienced the wisdom on these pages.

—Mickey Death

Artist

At a time when there is so much discussion, confusion, and even fear about the power and presence of the Holy Spirit and how believers deal with the reality of spiritual warfare, Michelle's gentle voice rings clear. Her down-to-earth and practical explanations, along with biblically sound principles, demystify and bring clarity to this often-misunderstood part of our spiritual journey. I found myself almost unable to put it down once I started. Simply a great addition to my library.

—Rev. Dr. Kenneth DeMaere

HOPE FOR THE WEARY,

DISAPPOINTED,

DEVASTATED,

AND INDIFFERENT

FIERCE HOPE

Michelle Dwyer

FIERCE HOPE
Copyright © 2021 by Michelle Dwyer

Printed in Canada

Softcover ISBN: 978-1-4866-2199-6 | Hardcover ISBN: 978-1-4866-2201-6
eBook ISBN: 978-1-4866-2200-9

Word Alive Press
119 De Baets Street, Winnipeg, MB R2J 3R9
www.wordalivepress.ca

Cataloguing in Publication may be obtained through Library and Archives Canada

For Brian.

Thank you for loving me through the learning.

Thank you for your bold faith—
it gave me the space to write
and the courage to share it with the world.

Love you forever,
M

CONTENTS

For there is hope for a tree, when it is cut down, that it will sprout again, and its shoots will not fail. Though its roots grow old in the ground, and its stump dies in the dry soil, at the scent of water it will flourish and produce sprigs like a plant.

—Job 14:7–9, NASB

INTRODUCTION

As I've sat writing and rewriting these many words, I have pictured you, dear reader, sitting across the table from me with a beverage of choice. I've heard your stories in a multitude of different encounters and I long to tell you mine. I want you to know there's hope—so much hope.

Humans are deeply complex, a fusion of spirit, soul, and body. All the parts are interrelated. We know that exercising and eating healthy food have an impact on our thoughts and emotions. We know when we're grateful and look on the bright side, our bodies have more energy. The spiritual realm also has a huge impact on our physical and emotional experiences.

I'm going to share what I've learned about this intersection of the spiritual with the physical and emotional facets of our experiences. The things I share with you don't work separate from the other dimensions—and I would encourage you to consider everything you read in light of this. My story is descriptive, not prescriptive, but what I have learned along the way has helped countless people.

My whole healing journey has been about taking one small step after another. At no point was I given the blueprint. I didn't know what the finished product would look like—actually, I still don't know, but I can see the beautiful "bones" of this house and I love it. Everything the Architect of my soul has done so far to restore my being has enhanced the beauty.

This book is the blueprint I've recognized after the fact.

In the following pages I will tell you snippets of my story of losing and finding hope, share with you principles that changed my life, and give you tools to help you integrate these principles into your own life.

My story is mine, but I know it will help you. Once upon a time I was anxious and very insecure and now I am courageous and excited about being seen and known. I know who I am. I know that I'm deeply loved. The journey to this point was full of different encounters: friends, counsellors, books, workshops, retreats, and solitary moments of encounter with God.

My prayer is that this book will be a pitstop on your journey, releasing you from fetters that hold you back and limit your hope. The world is waiting for you and longing for the beauty that's inside you. You were created to live free and full of hope.

Most chapters end with a tool to activate this goodness in your life. The final section of each chapter is called Here's Hope. This section isn't about delivering information for your head, but rather inspiration for your heart. Don't skip over it. Pause. Breathe. Receive hope. Let it seep in. It will grow, chapter by chapter.

THE
OPENING ACT

Chapter One

All the world's a stage...
> —William Shakespeare, *As You Like It*

WE'RE ALL BORN A BIT OF A HOT MESS. LITERALLY AND FIGURATIVELY. I arrived on the scene in 1970, two weeks late in the humid dog days of a maritime August. Oh, and after two days of unsuccessful labour. Doctors saved the day—and my life. I entered the world to an unconscious mother and the absence of a father, as dads weren't invited into surgical suites in those days. I was lovingly swaddled by a nurse and tucked into a bassinet.

I was wanted and eventually celebrated. My mom returned to consciousness a couple of days later and the grainy black-and-white photos bear witness to her holding me close, weary but tender. My dad picked my name and bought cigars and celebrated with his buddies.

Yet a nagging sense of abandonment and insecurity has dogged me most of my life. How can this be when I was clearly loved and cared for?

We were born into a world at war, you and I. We were created for Eden—the pristine garden where God placed the first humans—but none of us were born there.

To start, the stage of my life was set with a loving but unconscious mother, a delighted father, a dedicated medical team, and a squalling seven and a half pounds of precious baby.

There were unseen forces present that had a significant impact, too. They were also present at your birth.

Allow me to introduce them to you.

The enemy of our souls was there, lurking, intent on stealing, killing, and destroying. He was there to rob me of my identity as precious, beloved, and worthy. Without this foundation, my destiny would be stunted at best and perhaps altogether thwarted. The Creator was there as well, singing and dancing and celebrating my coming. Heaven had been waiting for this masterpiece to arrive on the scene and display all the glory they had planned for me before a single rock had existed to form this planet. Angels were assigned to watch over me and my destiny (John 10:10, Zephaniah 3:17, Ephesians 1:4, Psalm 91:11).

Add to that the unseen generations that formed my heritage. I have good parents who always provided for my needs. I inherited good things just by virtue of being born into a hard-working and resilient family.

Yet they, too, were born into a world at war that inflicted wounds on them long before I showed up. Those wounds in turn affected the succeeding generation, just as mine have affected my children. You have probably seen this in your story, too.

Is there any hope for the human race?

HERE'S HOPE

You are holding this book in your hands because the answer is a resounding *yes*.

Darkness and Light

Chapter Two

The Life-Light blazed out of the darkness; the darkness couldn't put it out.

—John 1:5, MSG

MOST OF US HAVE SCATTERED MEMORIES OF OUR CHILDHOOD, AND ALL of us have a few intense memories. Those memories may seem random or insignificant. They might be painful or traumatic. They might be ones everyone in the family jokes about and which we wish they would forget.

Regardless of how we feel about those memories on the spectrum of joy or sadness, they are significant.

I remember an Easter egg hunt in a hotel room and feeling really special in a little blue dress and black patent shoes. I remember stirring mud puddles with the boy next door and thinking it looked exactly like stirring cream into coffee. I remember stealing carrots from the neighbour's garden with the same boy and our moms making us knock on the neighbour's door to apologize. I remember this ancient neighbour man accepting our apology and giving us mints. I had the sneaking suspicion he was laughing on the inside.

These memories remind me that I was loved, that I was part of a community, and that I had some really good training.

Two particular memories have marked my life like lightning strikes. One is good news and one is bad news. They reveal the presence of those unseen forces ever-present in our lives.

Since everyone always says they'd like the bad news first, I'll start there.

Around the time I was five, I was taken regularly to visit one set of my grandparents. Both grandparents were in the same mental hospital at the time—Bumpa in the men's wing and Grammy in the women's wing.

Nothing about this was a bad idea. Grandparents are important. They are worthy of love and care. A visit from a grandchild is a great opportunity for them to experience hope and a reason to live. The motivation for this particular visit was simply love.

I remember green hallways and a lot of sadness. I've always been incredibly sensitive to what other people are feeling. It turns out this is a gift, but it sure doesn't feel like it when you don't know what to do with it!

I remember standing next to my grandfather's bed. I remember an unpleasant smell. I remember the cubby holes in a shelf at the head of his bed. I *felt* darkness. I felt it crawl all over me and come to rest in my tummy.

The unseen ones whose sole purpose is to steal, kill, and destroy wanted another generation of my family. The fact that I was an innocent child and my loving parents had no idea of the spiritual forces at work meant nothing to these thieves. They were predators and I was prey. They wanted to rob me of emotional vitality, to torment me with fear and rejection.

From that time forward, I was conscious of a slightly sick feeling in my stomach, a baseline of fear and sadness all the time. I have a million other happy memories—there has been a lot of goodness in my life—but I only had to pause and check in and there it was, still deep in my tummy.

Until the day it wasn't anymore, but we'll get to that.

Now for the good news story!

About a year later, when I was six years old, I lay in bed on a humid summer night. The window was open and I could hear the neighbours socializing with their friends across our back yard. They were playing loud, raucous music that amped up the deep feeling of fear that generally lurked inside me.

By this time in my life, both of my parents had experienced the reality of Jesus and they had recently sent me to a week of Vacation Bible School. I'd been hearing a lot about Jesus.

As I lay restlessly in bed, unable to sleep from heat and anxiety, I thought to invite Jesus to come into my bed with me. So I did.

"Jesus, I'm afraid," I whispered. "Please come be with me."

Immediately I felt a warm, tangible presence and I wasn't afraid anymore. It was the most wonderful thing I had ever experienced. I scooted over to the very edge of my bed to make room for Him, whispered that I wanted Him to stay with me forever, and went to sleep.

I have never doubted His presence since. I've been rebellious against it. I've been annoyed with His failure to act how and when I want Him to, but I've never doubted that He is real and that ultimately the sense of His presence will calm all my fears.

These two events have defined my whole life. For years, that lurking darkness was like an unseen haemorrhage. It eventually became a place of triumph that fuels my passion to spread hope. The very real presence of Jesus has been my anchor. He's the One who ultimately delivered me fully from that darkness.

However, there was a long and confusing period of paradox. Can someone know and love Jesus, have a pretty decent life, and yet still live with torment? One can argue about this philosophically or academically, but there's no argument in experience. Millions will tell you that this is their story. I'm about to share my pathway to wholeness, and I pray you will find treasures along the way that become a catalyst for your own freedom.

You also have a story of defining moments. Some may have seemed insignificant at the time, but they've marked your life. Before we go any further, I would encourage you to pause and allow your early memories to surface. Do this without edit or judgment.

Remain curious. If you know some memories are lurking, but you don't want to fully look at them, that's okay. Just make note of them. You don't have to "go there" now.

It has been my observation and experience that regardless of how great or abysmal an individual's life has been, the enemy has come to wreak havoc at certain times, and the love of God has been revealed at others. My desire is to help everyone reclaim what has been lost and live fully defined by that great and glorious love. The fact that you're holding this book in your hands is proof that God has not abandoned you to torment.

Hope is a matter of the head and heart. In the following chapters, you will find stories and strategies that lead you through a process of addressing the darkness that has blocked the light of hope. I've shared these truths and strategies with thousands of people, and every time I've seen light break in. They will do the same for you because the One who has loved me so relentlessly loves you, too, and is fully invested in your freedom, no matter how great your sadness.

HERE'S HOPE

There is hope for you and your story... a hope that is real and solid, more than a flighty feeling that comes and goes. It's an expectation of goodness that is rooted in knowing that you're deeply loved and that there is a good plan for your life.

Take a deep breath and dare to believe it might be possible.

THE
GREAT SADNESS

Chapter Three

*Lord, why do you seem so far away when evil is near? Why have
you hidden yourself when I need you the most?*
—King David, c. 1000 B.C. (Psalm 10:1, TPT)

WHEN I WAS NINE YEARS OLD, THE SEASON OF GREAT SADNESS BEGAN
in our family. First, my mom's best friend died of cancer even though we
had prayed and believed, and prayed and believed some more, that she
would be healed.

Despite the sadness, I still knew the comforting presence of Jesus.
He was with me and I knew without a doubt that He loved "Auntie" Ren,
too. We were all really sad when she died, but I was still quite young and
kids are resilient.

Then my uncle and aunt and baby cousin were killed in a head-on
collision by a drunk driver. It was all so sudden and confusing… the phone
ringing, my mom collapsing on the floor in shock and grief. I remember
her drawing on some deep mother-strength and pulling us in close and
trying to explain the unexplainable.

One thing I began to understand: tragedy can strike at any moment.
You can be playing with your little sister one moment and death can come
crashing in without warning the next.

I began to draw some conclusions about life. People are going to be
very sad and it's my job to be very good and not cause more problems—
even better if I can be extra kind and make them feel better. Death might
come crashing in, but at least people could count on Michelle to be nice.

The avalanche of sadness didn't stop there. My Opa died of cancer a few months later after a long, slow sickness.

I loved being at my grandparents' farm. It was a happy place of apple blossoms, milk cows, and sweet-smelling manure. And my Oma was my epicentre of nurture. I felt cherished by her—even if she did laugh till she cried the day I tried to help with milking and got baptized in cow urine. She always lit up when I came into the room.

But now the farm became a place of sadness, too. I saw my dad cry for the first time—my strong, laughing dad who could fix everything. Except this.

In the wake of this loss, my mentally ill grandfather moved into our house for a while. His dark, brooding, smelly presence on the couch seemed a physical manifestation of the hopelessness that was becoming so much harder to resist.

I still knew Jesus was there. I could sometimes feel Him. Yet a lot of other feelings were very strong.

It got worse. The sleeping giant of mental illness stirred, getting ready to roar again.

One of my cousins had often been troubled. Sometimes he stayed with us, and I liked him a lot. He was kind of like the older brother I had always wanted. He was creative, an artist, a skilled woodworker, played classical guitar, and best of all, for a teen with a health-food-loving mother, he smuggled chocolate bars to me. When he was with us, I knew he wasn't okay, but I felt compassion toward him and no fear. He was always kind and gentle toward me.

One day, he went missing. Again. Some guns and food had been stolen from the cabin next to our family cottage. The owner suspected my cousin and contacted Uncle Gerry, my mom's youngest and obviously favourite brother.

My family became concerned that this cousin was unstable and there might be a risk of violence. I knew this even though all the adults discussed it in hushed whispers.

Gerry thought he'd try to get to him before the police did and hopefully talk him into turning himself in. Instead my cousin shot and killed my uncle. Point blank.

There are no words to describe the effect of this shock and horror. A literal, physical wail tore through us. Chaos and confusion. This couldn't be happening. It was as though the ground disappeared beneath us. As though the world was suddenly devoid of oxygen.

A funeral. A manhunt. Our name in the news. Hot shame. Whispering friends. Fatherless baby cousins. My mom utterly gutted by shock and loss. Pain. Sorrow. Disorientation. So many tears.

Then there was one more death within just a couple of weeks. My grandfather passed away quite suddenly from a heart attack, or perhaps a broken heart. Fractured relationships make grief complicated.

The enemy of our souls was roaring, claiming victory. Proving that there was no hope. No place of safety. Certainly no God who cared.

I knew that wasn't true. My Uncle Gerry had staked his life on the goodness of God and would have wanted me to do the same.

But it felt less and less real.

Seven traumatic deaths in five years. Five preteen/early teen years.

Fourteen is a tough age for anyone, with so many new feelings and ideas to sort through. It's easy to lose one's mooring, and I was especially vulnerable in all this chaos, but I never doubted the warm presence of Jesus that came over me and calmed my fears. At the same time, I didn't know what to do with that cloud of darkness in my tummy that felt like it was getting bigger.

The enemy of our soul always attaches his lies to facts. He whispered to me, saying that God wasn't good. It seemed true. Sadness and loss seemed bigger and truer than love and safety. God certainly didn't seem worth following if He wasn't going to do better than this.

HERE'S HOPE

This is not the end of the story.

The darkness was thick, lurking in every quiet and lonely moment.

There was also light. If the enemy of my soul was hellbent on destruction, the host of heaven was even more fierce about my healing.

Darkness doesn't have a chance against light.

NOT YOUR FAIRY
GODMOTHER

Chapter Four

Sadness is but a wall between two gardens.[1]

—Kahlil Gibran

RANDOMLY INTERVIEW A DOZEN PEOPLE ON THE STREET AND YOU'LL find out it's true: humans struggle to believe in a good God because of the pain they see and experience. This echoes the lie that Adam and Eve bought way back in the garden of Eden. The tempter baits us with the alluring fruit of human wisdom that disavows the goodness of God. At some point, every single one of us has bought the lie.

It can be subtle. Many high-functioning people live joyless lives because layers of disappointment have stolen their hopes and dreams of how they thought life would be. They check out in their work or entertainment and live safely unexpectant lives, believing they are slightly better than those who are obviously a mess.

Others live more blatantly broken. Their pain leaks out in obvious dysfunction. It can show up a million different ways and is so common that it often seems normal. They leave a trail of broken relationships. Secret and not-so-secret addictions. They grasp for love, money, or power. Anything to medicate the pain.

At sixteen, I gave up. I bought the lie. Faith was hard. Others were clearly having more fun. God had utterly abandoned me in sadness and loss, so why not join everyone else in the good times? I said yes to the nice-yet-wrong-for-me guy and did everything I could to drown my sorrows. I gave it my best shot for four years.

I graduated from high school early, went to college, got a job, and looked like I had my crap together. I was smart and funny and knew how to get along with people, so I did well in work and life. I enjoyed living on my own, at arm's length from my family's sadness. I got engaged to someone who I felt adored me.

If only that hidden sadness deep inside didn't keep me awake at night and ever-anxious. Afraid of messing up and being abandoned. Dreading all the what-ifs. Avoiding conflict. Feeling responsible for everyone and their happiness.

And I missed Jesus.

I knew He hadn't gone anywhere. He was still there. I remember sitting in a theatre—a no-no in my teen years—and having a sudden awareness that Jesus was present with me. How could He be when I was somewhere I'd been told He didn't want me to be? But I knew that Presence. I had experienced it numerous times.

Another time I sat in a bar, dressed up and feeling pretty hot. I tossed my head back in laughter, then looked down. My bracelet caught my eye. My parents had given it to me. It had my name engraved on it, but the nameplate had flipped over and there was a text engraved on the other side, the same text they had inscribed in my first Bible. I knew it well: *"Trust in the Lord with all your heart... don't lean on your own understanding..."* (Proverbs 3:5–6).

It was as shocking as an unexpected kiss!

Why? I asked God. *Why are You here talking to me when I'm trying so desperately to give You the finger? You've let me down horribly and I don't want anything to do with You!*

I was hiding from Him and He was calling my name, kind of like Adam and Eve did way back in the garden of Eden. Like them, I was shrouded in shame from having blatantly rejected Him with all my angry, trauma-driven choices. Layers of pain, disappointment, and confusion laminated my life. I was longing for Him and at the same time didn't want to give up my own ways. They were safe and comfortable. Known.

On the other hand, He was still a mystery. If He was so good, why was the world such a mess? Especially my world.

I wrestled, one sleepless night after another, for months. If I was going to say yes to Him again, I knew I would have to surrender all the things I was using to cushion my soul. There was nothing inherently wrong with the guy or my job. It's just that they were choices made in defiance of what I believed I should be doing. I had known since I was a little girl that I had a significant destiny and that God had adventures in store for me. Somehow I still believed, in spite of all the disappointment, that if I put God first He would satisfy the desires of my heart.

Sometimes the heart knows a truth that defies the rational mind.

Finally I surrendered. I decided that I would rather live in the tension of the mystery than the absence of His presence. On my twentieth birthday, I gave God my unequivocal no-turning-back yes. He would be Lord of my life even if He refused to be my fairy godmother and magically fix everything that was broken and disordered. It was going to be on His terms, not mine.

I went through a painful season of unravelling my self-willed choices—a broken engagement, a big move across the country, and a fresh start. Yet it was all wrapped in the tenderness and compassion of Jesus. Rather than punish me, He helped me.

The joy of His presence gave me the courage and strength I needed. Just like Job in the Bible, I found comfort and strength not in perfect circumstances, magically released through a bippity-boppity-boo moment, but through an encounter with God.

If you aren't familiar with the story of Job, let me refresh you.

HERE'S HOPE

Surrender makes space for fresh hope. The terrifying process of letting go empties our hands and frees us up to receive goodness.

THE
WHY TRAP

Chapter Five

I pray to the God within me that he will give me the strength to ask Him the right questions.[2]

—Elie Wiesel, *Night*

THE BIBLE RECORDS THE STORY OF A MAN NAMED JOB. I DON'T KNOW if this story is historical or metaphorical but it has given me much to ponder. Job was shockingly rich. He had ten kids, which was considered a bonus in those days. He owned seven thousand sheep, three thousand camels, five hundred teams of oxen, and five hundred donkeys—basically the equivalent of stocks, bonds, and oil wells. He had countless servants and was definitely the richest guy in town.

Yet he was unusual. He was a man of utter integrity who obeyed God completely. His family gathered regularly and worshiped God together.

As the story goes, Satan shows up in the courtroom of heaven and tells God that the only reason Job is so faithful and good is that he's got it made in life. If Job didn't have such a great life, he would surely curse God rather than obey Him.

God then gives Satan permission to test Job, but not to physically harm him.

It's as though a cyclone of disaster hits Job's life. Four messengers arrive, one after another, to deliver bad news. Marauding invaders have come and taken all the oxen and donkeys and killed all the farmhands. Fire has fallen from the sky and burned up all the sheep and shepherds. Raiders have stolen all the camels and killed the servants in charge of the herd.

Finally, the worst news of all: while Job's children were feasting in the oldest brother's home, the building collapsed and killed every one of them.

Job is overcome with grief. There are no words to describe the impact of this level of devastation. He tears his beautiful clothing, shaves his head, and falls to the ground. Yet as he lays there, he acknowledges that everything he had came from God—and if God chooses to take it away, Job will still worship Him.

Sometimes when we sit and read the stories in the Bible, it's easy to overlook timeframes. We have no idea how much time passes before Job is tested even further. How long did he sit in this unresolved grief yet continue to acknowledge God as the Lord of his life?

After an undefined length of time, there is another convening in heaven. Satan acknowledges that Job has maintained his integrity throughout this devastating loss, but that's only because he still has his health. If Job were to lose his health, surely he would curse God! So God gives permission for Satan to attack Job's health as well, but he must not take Job's life.

Job is struck with boils from head to toe. He sits among the ashes, scraping his skin with a piece of broken pottery. His wife then comes along and adds insult to injury by mocking Job for his refusal to curse God in all his pain. With this, Job's only remaining family member has turned on him. He is utterly bereft. There is nothing left but the breath in his lungs—and he uses that breath to continue worshiping.

Job has three friends who come along and sit with him, trying to help him make sense of what's going on. I have no doubt they are well intentioned; they are often referred to as Job's comforters, though perhaps somewhat sarcastically. They contribute the best of their human wisdom, which boils down to the fact that this is somehow all Job's fault—he is being punished.

Job will have none of it. He hotly defends himself and expresses confusion. He doesn't know why this is happening, but he refuses to accuse God. He proclaims, "*God might kill me, but I have no other hope*" (Job 13:15). Job clings to God in the tension of the mystery.

I will admit that when I read these *thirty-four* chapters of human wisdom, I'm often confused. What these friends say makes so much sense to me! I have to remind myself that God eventually shows up and reveals that they've got it all wrong. In fact, God is angry with them because they haven't spoken accurately about Him. Though there are nuggets of wisdom along the way, their human rationale never discovers the truth of what's actually going on. As far as we know, Job himself never knows the whole story.

In fact, not a single question gets answered.

That's awkward! How on earth are we supposed to resolve things without answers?

Resolution comes when Job has an encounter with God. In the thirty-eighth chapter, God shows up and answers him *"from the whirlwind"* (Job 38:1). This is kind of a funny statement. as God doesn't *answer* a single question. Rather, He asks a lot of questions, such as *"Where were you when I laid the foundations of the earth?"* (Job 38:4) and *"Have you given the horse its strength or clothed its neck with a flowing mane?"* (Job 39:19) For two chapters, the beauty, majesty, and mystery of God and His creation are put on display.

Then God pauses and offers a particularly challenging question: *"You are God's critic, but do you have the answers?"* (Job 40:2)

Ouch. That question ricochets through me like a pinball. Am I a critic of God with no answers? Are you?

Job replies, *"I am nothing—how could I ever find the answers? I will cover my mouth with my hand. I have said too much already. I have nothing more to say"* (Job 40:3–5). I feel it every time I read it: "I have said too much already." Indeed I have.

Then God goes on. This encounter is intense! Relentless. He challenges Job, *"Brace yourself like a man, because I have some questions for you, and you must answer them"* (Job 40:7).

What do you do when God Almighty challenges you to take it like a man? I don't sense that God is cruel in this encounter, but He is fierce. Truth encounters can be like that.

Two more chapters ask impossible questions and proclaim the beauty and power of the Creator. Finally it comes to an end and Job is undone: *"I had only heard about you before, but now I have seen you with my own eyes"* (Job 42:5).

There is so much tension and mystery in this. It's uncomfortable but powerful.

Job wanted answers, but what he needed was an encounter. His kids were still gone, his stuff was destroyed, and his body was covered in boils, yet he came to a place of quietness and peace. Not a single question had been answered, but He encountered the greatness and beauty of God and his soul was at rest.

The story concludes with God reprimanding Job's friends, Job praying for them, and his health and fortunes being restored. There's no replacement of what was lost, but there is restoration.

I've just summarized a story that took a significant span of time to live through. Job's suffering and loss were very real. His struggle to gain understanding and resolution is natural to humans. Our brains are wired to make sense of things.

The point, however, is this: peace came to Job through an encounter with God, not through satisfying answers.

God's challenge to Job was, *"You are God's critic, but do you have the answers?"* (Job 40:2) Indeed. I think we have all been that critic. Seldom have we found the answers, and even less often have those answers been accurate. The endless quest for them seems like a solution for our pain, yet it's rarely found. Is there no other comfort?

We cannot have an authentic conversation about hope without acknowledging that there is unresolved mystery around suffering. Can we live in the tension of that mystery and still have hope?

Thankfully, few of us have experienced calamity in the overwhelming proportions Job did, but we have all experienced pain, loss, and disappointment.

Frankly, I don't like Job's story—nor do I like the trauma in mine—but I offer this detour into Job's narrative as an insight into how I've made peace with the tension of the unexplainable. That which I cannot understand, I can surrender to a God who is knowable yet much bigger than my understanding. Perhaps someday we will be able to make sense of things that are currently beyond our comprehension, but that's small comfort right now. In order to move forward in hope, we must accept some mystery. I don't think this is a copout. I think it's wisdom.

As you consider the wreckage of disappointment in your own life, it's perfectly natural to wonder why these things have happened. Rarely are these questions answered, which can lead us into the trap of asking "Why!?" This can become the cry of the victim. In this place, our loss defines us and our lack of answers traps us. Pay attention to this cry and consider changing the question to "Where? Where are You, God? Will You show me Your presence?"

Shifting the question from *why* to *where* might change your life.

In a future chapter, we're going to cover more about finding God's presence in your story. But for now, you can start by applying some tools.

THE TOOL

Surrender the whys and ask God to show you His presence in the midst of your struggle. He is there. He is with you.

The idea of surrendering your right to understand can stir up feelings of rebellion. My need to demand "Why?" was often an angry fist raised to the face of God.

Learn from Job. Thirty-seven chapters of flailing got him nowhere.

Choose wisdom. Acknowledge the tension of the mystery. Receive peace.

HERE'S HOPE

He is near to the broken-hearted. He will never leave you or abandon you. He feels your pain and is totally invested in restoring everything that has been lost, stolen, and broken. He is Saviour, healer, and deliverer.

Hold your questions before God, but seek His face. Knowing the comfort of His presence will sustain you in the tension of the mystery.

There will be more restoration in the chapters to come.

BABY STEPS

Chapter Six

A journey of a thousand miles begins with one step.[3]

—Lao Tzu

I MOVED FROM THE EAST COAST TO THE WEST COAST TO START A FRESH
life. I knew the choices I had made weren't sustainable without a total
change of environment. This was a wonderful new beginning for me, as it
renewed my sense of joy and connection to Jesus. I had finally resolved my
long period of wrestling with my will, and it was such a relief.

It was also a season of great loss. I had ended a four-year relationship
and moved to an unknown place and unknown people. I was in the same
country, yet found myself in a very different culture.

I'd left a job I loved as a legal assistant in a firm that had been keen
to support my goal of becoming a lawyer. I was an avid observer of current events and often thought of entering the political world as a way to
influence people for good. I had moved to an area where the economy was
based on forestry and mining—subjects I knew absolutely nothing about.
I felt like a stranger in a strange land. I didn't understand half the lingo
my peers used and when I tried to start conversations about matters that
interested me, I was met with blank stares. I felt very lonely.

While I loved my relationship with Jesus, I was also grieving the loss
of human friendships and intimacy.

Any time we experience loss, there is a ripping and tearing of our
souls, leaving behind a raw wound that's vulnerable to infection. While I
finally experienced amazing peace, since I was no longer rebelling against
the great love of Jesus, I also experienced sadness and loneliness which

made me vulnerable to the ancient lies of fear and abandonment. Sadness came over me in great waves, threatening to drown me.

As time wore on and the joy of my fresh start became a relentless and unpleasant state of "ordinary," I began to feel as though I was losing the battle.

One evening, the sadness flattened me. It was as though the force of my will was no longer enough. My determination to do the right thing was all used up. I couldn't find Jesus beyond a mental acknowledgement that I knew He was there. I was on empty. I felt dead inside.

I lay on the floor in my living room, wondering what I was to do and how I was to survive. I had nothing left but that old sense of my soul haemorrhaging. There was no turning back and no clear way forward. I felt helpless and, yes, abandoned.

Jesus, You brought me here, I thought. *Now what? Take this sadness away! Please give me joy again!*

Nothing.

Nothing but deadness and silence.

I wanted it all to end. I wasn't suicidal, yet there seemed no escape other than death.

Jesus, if You aren't going to deliver me from this, then please take me home.

I lay there in the silence, hot tears running down into my ears. The weight of sadness was so overwhelming that I felt as though I had no physical strength to do anything. If He was so good, why wasn't He doing something about this?

That question again.

More silence.

I hadn't yet learned that I was asking the wrong question.

While I lay there, begging for reprieve, a little song seeped into the background of my awareness. It was a simple song from my childhood: "God is so good. God is so good. God is so good. He's so good to me." I felt a pang of irritation! If He was actually so good and I was being obedient to His will, then why was I feeling this way?

It was the old familiar lie again. He's distant. He doesn't care. I'm on my own.

This is exactly what had taken me out before, but I hadn't caught on yet. I wanted a way of escape, not a platitude.

The minutes ticked by with no resolution. The tears continued to fall as that little song kept whispering in the background.

It occurred to me that maybe this was somehow from God, not simply a random thought.

Seeing no other options, I began to whisper the words out loud. Then I sang them softly. My tears stopped and I was able to draw deep breaths. I sang the song again and then stood up, feeling life creep back into my soul.

I sang it again, louder, and began to feel it.

I sang it again and again.

The song went from a whisper to my loudest possible voice. It took on the tone of a battle cry. I marched around my house, singing in a powerful voice, "God is so good! He's so good to me!" Now I was laughing through my tears. I was sad, yet strong.

I felt as though I was fighting for my life.

In fact, I was.

What happened? I had aligned my soul and body with the truth: God is good. He was still good, though my circumstances were hard. I *encountered* Him and His goodness held me. My awareness of His presence amidst my pain became a tangible promise that there was goodness in store for me.

THE TOOL

This tool is simple but powerful. God wants you to know the peace of His presence right now. If you know this song, sing it. If you feel you can't sing it, hum it. If you don't know the song, whisper these simple words: "God is so good. God is so good. God is so good. He's so good to me."

Do it as a simple act of your will. Do it at least three times. And then keep going until you feel it seeping into your bones.

If this seems weird to you, think of it as an experiment. Be curious. Give it a try.

HERE'S HOPE

This isn't about denying your pain or the challenges you face. It's about a truth that is more powerful than feelings or circumstances.

It's recalibration.

ALIGNMENT

Chapter Seven

And when you align yourself with God's purpose as described in the Scriptures, something special happens to your life. You're in alignment.[4]

—Bono

GOD LOVES CHOICES. HE CREATED THE PARADISE OF EDEN AND GAVE its inhabitants a choice—eat all you want from the entire garden, but do not eat from this one tree.

Unfortunately, most of us have no idea what we're choosing. We don't even know we're making a choice. We live in tune with our drives and tangible circumstances, mostly oblivious to the unseen players on the stage of our lives.

In the beginning, Adam and Eve had it made. They had an abundance of peace, provision, and intimacy—absolutely everything required for them to flourish was available to them. There was just one thing they weren't supposed to do: eat from the tree of the knowledge of good and evil.

The enemy of their souls planted the idea that somehow God was holding out on them. After all, with virtually unlimited freedom, that one restriction really stood out. It would kind of get to you. You'd really ponder it. It could easily become an obsession.

One day they cratered and bought the lie. They exerted their godlike powers as commanders of their destiny and ate the forbidden fruit.

Nothing has ever been the same since.

Whether you consider the Garden of Eden story to be literal or metaphorical, the result is the same. Free will has opened Pandora's box. Humans decided that God was holding out on them, and so paradise was lost.

As a result, you and I have been born into a world at war. This war isn't between God and Satan or good and evil; rather, it's a war for our souls.

Through human will, paradise was lost. And through human will partnering with the grace of Jesus, paradise will be regained.

It starts with a gift of grace. Jesus Christ, the Son of God, laid aside His divinity to live like you and me—with human needs and desires as well as the power of choice. He chose to acknowledge the wisdom of God rather than be jerked around by the passions of human nature. He did this by leaning on the strength of the Holy Spirit, not merely through human willpower. Because of this, He lived a life completely without sin.

He was crucified, yet death couldn't hold Him down—three days later, He rose to life again. He then turned and offered the human race the gift of grace. He said that if we would believe and follow in His ways, then everything that was lost through Adam and Eve's crappy choice would be regained through the powerful sacrifice made by Jesus (Romans 5:12–21, Philippians 2:6–11).

Paradise lost and access regained.

Yet we all live in this world at war. No life has been left untouched. We see the devastation of evil and all experience loss. Depression, mental illness, anxiety, and suicide keep increasing. Hatred, abuse, and addiction continue to wreak havoc. Bodies, hearts, and minds are shattered by pain and the cycle continues.

Even those who have accessed this wonderful gift of grace often live as though there's very little difference in their experience of life here on earth. It's disheartening, to say the least. It often seems as though our best option for survival is to become numb.

The whole human race is eating from the tree of the knowledge of good and evil. We constantly make decisions about what's good and what isn't. I have a good day if nothing goes too far sideways. If my boss is cranky, my car breaks down, or my kids do something dumb, it's a bad day.

All day, every day, the enemy of our souls is whispering the suggestion that perhaps God isn't good and that He's holding out on us. When we agree with this lie from the enemy, we give him authority in our lives just like Adam and Eve did.

The enemy of their souls came to Adam and Eve in the form of a serpent described as crafty, sneaky, and cunning. He comes to you and me the same way. He always pairs his lies with the facts of our circumstances, facts that we can see and feel. When life piles up and God doesn't respond immediately as we think He should, we easily buy the lie that He's holding out on us.

Deceptive.

Believable.

Still a lie.

When the people we love reject us, we come to believe that we've been abandoned and are unworthy of love. When we compare ourselves to others, we believe we are insignificant. When we have suffered abuse, we wrap ourselves in shame. When we do something well and people approve of us, we think it makes us valuable or better than others.

These are identity lies. They tell us who we are and who we aren't. Because we're born into a world at war, these thoughts and ideas are imprinted onto our souls long before we start having conscious thoughts. Every one of these "agreements" allows a lie to form and shape us—or mis-shape us. As we live in reaction to them, or try to compensate for them, we become broken and deformed, a dim reflection of our original design, which was created to be powerful and free.

Other lies are circumstantial. We believe our situation is hopeless or that someone will never change. We experience fear, which makes us feel powerless, and we make an agreement that the world is no longer safe. We believe the lie that it's all up to us and we pick up control and manipulation. We use anger and deceit to get what we want.

Now we've made agreements with false protectors.

There is a truth that trumps facts.

People have rejected you, but God has not rejected you. You have made poor choices, but you are not unworthy of love. People have sometimes failed to recognize the gift that you are, but you are not insignificant. You have experienced loss and pain, but your situation is not hopeless. People have expected more of you than you have to give, but you are not responsible for the universe. You feel like you need to do more to hold your spot, but you are enough.

Now what?

We need to break agreement with these lies-that-feel-true and align ourselves with the truth that trumps the facts. The same gift of grace that made us right with God through the work of Jesus is abundantly available to restore our souls, not someday in the airy-fairy future, but today.

Try saying this out loud: "In the name of Jesus, I break every agreement I have made with the lie that I'm not loved. Jesus, I ask that You take this far away from me. What do You have for me instead?"

Where we have made an agreement with a lie, we must break agreement with that lie and make an agreement with the truth. Picture yourself fiercely tearing up the contract you've made with the enemy of your soul and writing a new one with Jesus. What is He offering you today? Love? Hope? Security? Peace? Confidence?

Wait in stillness to see what He has for you. He never leaves us empty-handed. He always trades up! You may sense peace, a bubble of joy, or a gentle warming. You may have a thought or idea pop into your mind. If it's a thought that brings a sense of lightness, joy, or peace, you can trust that it's from Jesus. However, if it feels dark and hopeless, fearful or condemning, you can know that it doesn't come from Jesus. It's simply another lie. We know this because the truth of the nature and character of God is that He brings light that dispels darkness. God *is* love. It is who He is and what He does.

Don't be dismayed if you don't get light and truth the first time you try this. The enemy doesn't want to give up territory in your heart and mind. This is worth fighting for!

I challenge you to lean in right now. Simply break agreement again, using this same declaration out loud, but breaking agreement with the fresh lie. The lie might be that you're unworthy, that God doesn't want to talk to you, or a general sense of confusion. Don't back down.

Say, "In the name of Jesus, I break every agreement I have made with the lie that I'm unworthy of hearing from God. I break agreement with shame... confusion... insignificance... Jesus, I ask You to take this far away from me. What do You have for me instead?"

If nothing else comes to mind, say it aloud: "I am deeply loved!" Do this until you sense peace.

Now take ownership of what Jesus is giving you! Write it down. Tell someone. Speak the truth out loud. As you own it, notice that you begin to *experience* it more deeply. This is both spiritual and physical. Neuroscience tells us that we can cut off thought patterns in our brains and lay tracks for new ones. Something very powerful and multidimensional is happening as you engage in this process.

When I began to declare that God is good, I rejected the lie that I had been abandoned to my difficult circumstances. I was aligning myself to the truth of God's goodness in the midst of my pain. When I stood up and began singing, I aligned my body and soul with the truth my spirit received when I first surrendered to the love of God. This alignment brings strength and health to our bodies. It brings clear thinking and calm to our minds and emotions. It energizes us for life. In those moments, I regained access to something of paradise—intimacy with God and joy in the awareness of His love for me.

Through this powerful declaration, I wasn't creating a reality. Rather, I was aligning myself to something that had been powerfully true all along. We're not just trying harder not to think or behave in a certain way; we are receiving catalytic truth that sets us on a new path.

You are deeply loved by God. You can neither earn nor lose this love. It's yours. He will never leave you. He is present to help you. This truth eclipses facts and circumstances.

People can be reluctant to engage in this process if they aren't sure how they feel about Jesus. Let me reassure you that you don't have to have yourself all sorted about Him before you give this a try. He is very sure about how He feels about you and He simply invites you to get to know Him.

Nowhere do we have a record of Him authoritatively commanding or demanding trust. Rather He says, *"Come to me... you will find rest for your souls"* (Matthew 11:28–29). Just as every relationship begins with a glance and a conversation, so you can get to know Jesus.

Perhaps you've had experiences with people that have left you with a sour taste in your mouth about Jesus. I encourage you to set those aside and get to know Him directly. Read the Gospel of John. It's the firsthand account of a man named John who hung out with Jesus for three years.

As you read the stories, imagine yourself in them. How does Jesus talk to people? Who does He stop for? What does He want them to know?

THE TOOL

Check yourself. Are you experiencing any toxic emotions or thoughts right now? They may be connected to real experiences or events but contain the essence of a lie that's blocking your ability to function well. Do your best to name it and then insert it into the following declaration, which should be said aloud: "In the name of Jesus, I break every agreement I have made with _____. Jesus, I ask that You take this far away from me. What do You have for me instead?

This is just a first step. There may be other things reinforcing these lies, but we'll get there in the pages to come!

HERE'S HOPE

Jesus is not pushy. He's simply offering you the invitation to a conversation. Give it a try. Use this tool. Don't rush on past this point.

Pause. Listen. Receive.

POWERFUL PICKING

Chapter Eight

Today I have given you the choice between life and death… Oh, that you would choose life, so that you and your descendants might live!
—Deuteronomy 30:19

I'VE BEEN BLESSED WITH THREE DELIGHTFUL CHILDREN. EVERY single one of them is strong-willed. I remember hearing a statistic that one in four children is compliant, but clearly I stopped short of the compliant one.

I found parenting incredibly challenging when they were preschoolers. I was raised in the era of obey-me-or-else—and the or-else usually involved a wooden spoon on the backside. It was pretty effective on me, but I felt like I was in a constant power struggle with my kids and I hated it.

I came across a book that encouraged raising powerful kids by making them aware of choices and consequences, letting them choose, and then following through. I thought it was worth a try even though some of my friends told me I was crazy—according to them, I needed to show those kids who was the boss!

Yet I had a sneaking suspicion that my firstborn had a stronger will than I and that she was going to eventually win this whole power struggle.

One day I asked her to do something—probably pick up her toys. She turned immediately defiant. I calmly let her know that she could pick up her toys or not, it was her choice, but if she didn't she would not get to watch her favourite show that day. She didn't hesitate to take the confrontation to the next level.

Even though she wanted to fight me on that, I simply returned to the task I had been doing. She didn't like that at all. She tried to engage me again.

"It's okay," I gently replied. "You get to pick."

She tried to engage me in a debate several more times, but I calmly and quietly told her every time that she could pick.[5]

She hardly knew what to do. Then she got really angry. Balling her little fists and stomping her foot, she yelled, "I no wanna pick!"

Then she dissolved into a little puddle. I sat on the floor with her and held her and told her she was a very powerful person and would always get to pick. Some choices would lead to good things and others would lead to hard things, but God made us free to choose.

It was easier for her to make me the enemy than to acknowledge that she was very much in charge of some of the outcomes in her life. So it is for all of us. It's easier to wallow as a victim of our circumstances than to rise up, fight the inertia, and powerfully choose to align ourselves with truth.

Many times I've recognized the three-year-old within myself yelling, "I no wanna pick!" I would much rather God show up as my fairy godmother and magically change my circumstances. When He doesn't, I'm inclined to withdraw into a hopeless space believing that I'm a victim and life simply sucks.

I know there will be readers who cannot relate to feeling like a victim at all. Perhaps you feel strong and impervious to pain. You've worked hard to prove you are powerful and successful. God hasn't shown up the way you would like Him to, but you are proving that you don't need Him. Yet this drive comes at a cost; it inoculates against the dark realities of the soul. Perhaps you've armed yourself with anger or hardness while defiantly resisting God's authority in your life.

Remember that the battle is for your soul. Your enemy would love nothing more than to have you rendered weak and powerless under the weight of shame, disappointment, rejection, hopelessness, insignificance, anxiety, and abandonment. If that doesn't appeal to your soul, he will be equally delighted to lure you into a false sense of power through pride, performance, bitterness, anger, control, and the lie that you don't need anyone.

Regardless of whether you have a posture of victimhood or bravado, there's a haemorrhage in your soul if you don't address these underlying realities.

Recognizing these powerful choices can be tricky in the beginning. Our reactions are hardwired from long before we even had the ability to read. When we were physically small, with developing hearts and minds, we learned to default to choices that made us feel safe. For some of us, safety meant making ourselves small and nonthreatening. Others learn to survive by bending others to their will.

Neither of these leads us to flourish.

You were created by design to be a powerful agent of choice. God gave you the beautiful gift of free will so you could make the world around you a place of goodness.

The enemy of our souls hates this so much. He knows how dangerous we are when we're aligned with the truth of who we were created to be. He's trying to lure you into either victim apathy or "brave" rebellion.

However, the Spirit of God is also present. He is tender toward you, inviting you to align yourself with truth that will set you free. Which will you choose?

Breaking our agreement with the lies that assault our souls isn't a magic bullet that instantly fixes everything, but it shifts the trajectory of our lives.

Science has shown us that it takes a minimum of twenty-one days of consistency to change a thought pattern in our brains.[6] You may need to break agreement with the same lie many times and reaffirm what Jesus has said to be true before this truth becomes your default. Whether you need to grow a "choosing muscle" or retrain the one you have, you are so powerful in this! No one can do it for you and no one can stop you from doing it. You get to pick!

This whole restoration process is about getting back to the truth about ourselves and our circumstances as proclaimed by our Creator— and then we can learn how to live in a new way.

I'm currently writing at a desk that my husband restored. It was a teacher's desk made in the early 1960s. He brought it home from a renovation he was working on because his clients were going to haul it to the dump.

Which is where I thought it belonged. The first time I saw it, there was rotting pizza and trash on top of it, along with what looked like years of filth where the protective finish had long ago worn off. The drawers were stained with who knows what. I didn't want to know. I wanted to burn it rather than touch it.

It was absolutely true that the desk had been abused. It was absolutely true that it was filthy. And it was true that under all that crap, there was beauty. It needed the eyes of a creator to see it, fight for it, work for it, and unveil it.

That is my husband. He spent countless hours refinishing it. He didn't use a sledgehammer; he was patient and gentle, careful to remove each layer of gunk in a way that wouldn't damage the beauty underneath.

The day he brought it into the house and set it up for me, I wept. It was so beautiful, with no trace of the former stains. He sanded the top to a velvety finish, rubbed in oil until the wood glowed, and added a protective coating. Honestly, I think it's far more lovely than a brand-new desk. My husband's tender loving care has increased its value.

It would have been the weirdest thing to bring it into the house in its former state, bizarre to enshrine the mess of it in any way. I wouldn't have been able to use it for its intended purpose.

Yet this is what happens when we prefer to hang on to the facts of what happened to us rather than work through the restoration process.

To restore something is to return it to its original condition. It's about seeing the beauty worth fighting for and working to unveil it.

You are worth fighting for. You are worth the effort. You can trust the gentle hands of your Creator. He will patiently deal with one layer at a time. You may want Him to hurry and get it over with, but He cherishes you and knows how much you can handle. It won't be comfortable, but it will be worth it.

One of the major strategies of the enemy is to continually repeat his lies as though that makes them true. Recognizing this is key: repetition of a lie doesn't make it true! Be fierce in clinging to truth. Spend time with truth speakers. Connect regularly with Jesus, who will lead you and guide you into more and more truth.

THE TOOL

Consider where you land on the spectrum of victim to bravado or bully. Do you tend to melt or power up in the face of challenges, conflict, or difficulty? Acknowledging your bent will alert you to potholes in your soul and the lies that are easy for you to believe. As you deliberately choose to align yourself with the truth of what Jesus is giving you, your soul will bend less in this direction and become more healthy and beautiful.

HERE'S HOPE

There is also healing for the wounds in which the lies fester. It's a good thing to break agreement with lies, but even better to address the wound that attracts the lies in the first place. Sometimes the choices you face are so hard because the lies have found a place to land in an old wound.

SWATTING FLIES

Chapter Nine

Dead flies cause the oil of the perfumer to send forth an evil odour.
— Ecclesiastes 10:1, ASV

IF YOU'VE EVER GONE HIKING OR CAMPING, YOU KNOW THAT
endlessly swatting flies can become tiresome and annoying.

Myiasis is a parasitic infection that sets in when a certain type of fly
lays its eggs in a body's open wounds. When these eggs hatch, the larvae
feed on the tissue of the host.

This is an incredibly repulsive thought, yet it's exactly what happens
to our souls. We were all born into a world at war and have taken hits.
Metaphorical flies are drawn to these wounds and they have one purpose:
exploit the host. They erode the host's health and, left untreated, ultimately bring destruction.

Interestingly, Wikipedia notes that myiasis in humans is often found
in neglected wounds, especially where there are predisposing conditions
such as "poor socioeconomic conditions, extremes of age, neglect, mental disability, psychiatric illness, alcoholism..."[7] These physical conditions
also predispose us to suffer deep wounds of the soul. Though the enemy
strikes in all places and spaces, it seems he has even more material to work
with in these conditions. We are even more vulnerable when we're raised
around other people's untreated wounds.

Even if you didn't experience these specific conditions while growing up, you aren't exempt from being assaulted by the swarming flies
of this beautiful, broken earth. I have yet to meet anyone who hasn't
experienced rejection in some form or been motivated by fear in some

counterproductive way. All humans seem to be susceptible to the idea that they need to prove their value or worth by their performance or behaviour.

Everyone has experienced disappointment. At best, you have minor cuts and abrasions. At worst, you've been gutted. Either way, you are vulnerable to infection.

Most of us know enough pop psychology to realize there are obvious patterns of brokenness in the human race. Wounds that create more wounds. Those who've been sexually abused in childhood are more likely to use drugs or live a promiscuous lifestyle, which in turn causes pain to others. Those raised in anger are more likely to become angry adults, etc.

Not all wounds are so obvious, yet all are worthy of a healing encounter with God. He doesn't grade your pain on a sliding scale. You are His precious creation, and where damage has been done He is all about restoring it down to the finest detail. He cares about every facet of your life.

The first step is acknowledging that we have wounds. For some, this is easy. You're bleeding all over the place and you know it! However, others may feel they're quite high-functioning—and by any human standard, they are.

Yet the fact remains that we are all casualties of this war for our souls.

I knew a man who often seemed sad, tired, and irritable. He was always striving, as though nothing he did was quite good enough. He had grown up without a father teaching him and fighting for him. The deep wounds in his soul had left him living as though he wasn't loved, like he needed to prove himself and couldn't really count on anyone.

This drive made him hard-working and successful in some areas of his life, but pain and self-protection made it hard for him to experience meaningful connection in his relationships. Sometimes his family experienced him as uncaring and indifferent, multiplying his brokenness in the lives of those he loved as they began to live under the lie of not being loved or good enough. Only when he recognized the impact on his family did he find the courage and motivation to address his own pain.

I have a friend who once had one of the flattest personalities I'd ever encountered. She prided herself on being "level," thinking she was immune to these parasitic infections because her life didn't contain any notable trauma. She thought that was just the way she was, and it was fine.[8]

However, she got curious about the things I was teaching and one day she asked Jesus to show her if there were any untreated wounds in her soul. Two memories came to mind: one of being overlooked for a part in a play and the other of making the same silly but costly mistake twice. Fairly innocuous events, not uncommon in the human experience. This seemed like a frustrating answer to her prayer.

As we talked about it, she began to see that there was pain and shame in those events that led her to protect herself from disappointment. Out of this pain, she made a vow to never take risks. Without dreams or anticipation, she became safely boring.

When she saw this for what it really was, she realized that she wasn't safe at all. This no-risk posture was having a negative effect on her marriage and robbing her of her potential. She had to break agreement with the lies that told her she was insignificant, that life would be better when there was no risk of failure, and then face the disappointments she had safely and tidily labelled as no big deal.

Your brokenness is contagious. It has a way of multiplying pain in the lives of those in your proximity. These hidden and unaddressed toxins create more casualties.

Thankfully, the opposite is also true: health is contagious. Healthy people release love and hope, justice and courage, wherever they go. They make space for others to grow in health.

Only when I reached the end of my rope, recognizing that my coping skills weren't going to cut it and my marriage and children would be negatively affected, did I dive deeply into the hard work of healing. I was worth it, but I hadn't had the courage to do it for my own sake.

I realized that one way or another I was leaving a legacy for my kids. I could leave it to them to deal with the consequences of my dysfunctional ways of coping or I could be an example of someone who wildly pursues everything God has for me.

I could have just chosen to medicate my pain and carry on. But there's something fierce in the human spirit that knows it was designed for so much more.

In my own story, certain wounds were obvious. I had endured multiple tragedies at a formative time in my life. I was also born into generations of mental illness induced by rejection and abuse. Even though I hadn't experienced the same abuse my grandmother had, the statistical likelihood of my continuing in that pattern of mental illness was very high! Basic math.

The message of hope on these pages is that there is a redemption plan that trumps statistical likelihoods. The end of your story is not yet written!

It's an act of fierce courage to address the wounds in your story. It's an act of valour to set aside denial and coping mechanisms, to lay down your armour so you can take a good look at your wounds. It helps to do it in the kind presence of Jesus. His Spirit is with you right now, whispering hope. A good counsellor and supportive friends are also helpful in this process.

Choosing to uncover our wounds is counterintuitive. They are messy. They smell. It can be incredibly painful. We may have told ourselves that these wounds are barely noticeable and now we must admit to having them. It is awkward and humbling. We cannot heal ourselves.

THE TOOL

Acknowledge that there is room for healing in your life. Take an analytical inventory of your wounds as if you were doing triage on someone else. If you think you don't have any, get curious and ask Jesus to reveal anything you are unaware of. It's not necessary to dig up stuff, but it's helpful to humbly acknowledge that there is room to grow in self-awareness.

Don't settle for being "fine."

HERE'S HOPE

It will be messy, but it will be worth it. Your entire future will look different because you had the courage to pursue healing. Future generations of your family will be impacted because you thought freedom and health were worth fighting for.

Would you dare to ask your Creator to show you the wounds in your soul He would like to heal? Before you can go any further in this process, these need to be named. It's okay if you cannot handle all of them at once. Jesus is gentle. He will highlight a starting place. He only shows us so we can be restored.

I bless you with all the courage you need.

Raining
Toilets

Chapter Ten

Our masks have become our reality, and we have become our lies.[9]
—David G. Benner

I'm not one of those impressive women who know how to run power tools and mitre corners on their own handmade chalkboard frames. I can, however, slap a coat of paint on a wall—and do a good job, too. That is my idea of a renovation.

A few years ago, we were unable to travel in the summer so I took some time off work to paint my kitchen from its deep rusty barn red, trendy during the 2000s, to a soothing and more current blue-grey. It was a ton of work. I had to move all the junk and scrub all the gunk. I climbed up and down a million times. Three days later, I had the satisfaction of stepping back and admiring a kitchen that looked like new. It was a bit of work but totally worth it.

Some of our self-care looks like this, too. We can start a new exercise program or decide that it's time to read more books. We can recognize that we need to stop a bad habit, like chewing our nails or interrupting people in a conversation. All worthwhile ventures. Like a coat of fresh paint, they are an improvement.

Behaviour modification is a good idea, but it has its limitations. Some things are beyond mere modification. Much more than a fresh coat of paint is required. A total renovation is in order.

I have a friend who knew her toilet was a bit leaky, but she didn't think it was a big deal until the day it nearly fell through the rotting floor to the basement. She had even put down fresh linoleum not too long before that and noticed that the floor looked a little gross, but nothing a little fresh lino wouldn't fix!

Until the day the toilet took a dive. Then it became priority one.

Our lives can be like this. We can be pretty high-functioning and look like we have our stuff more or less together. Then one day the proverbial straw breaks the camel's back. A tsunami hits our lives. The toilet falls through the floor. It becomes undeniable that we're beyond the help of a mere coat of paint.

There's a gift in the rubble of these moments.

For me, this "toilet dive" came in the form of a perfect storm of postpartum challenges. I had the amazing gift of three preschoolers, but I was completely overwhelmed. Our marriage was stressed and the pressure revealed the need for renovation. My hormones were all over the place. I was sleep-deprived. I wasn't okay.

And it had never mattered more; I didn't want to totally screw up my kids.

All my coping mechanisms were insufficient. All my strategies for staying calm, cool, and collected had utterly failed me. I wasn't fine. I was a mess. And I was very afraid.

These moments eventually occur in all our lives. Our spouse walks out. We get a terrible diagnosis. We lose our job. Some may never have what could be described as a big trauma, but they may deal with anxiety or depression beyond their ability to manage. They despair as they realize that they cannot control their universe. Others simply resign themselves to living joyless lives devoid of adventure.

This can go two ways: you can up the ante by coping harder or you can get to the root of the issue. One is easier in the moment; the other is so much better in the long run.

When I was overwhelmed, I realized I could either become a closet alcoholic or hurl myself on Jesus. I chose the latter. It was a long journey, messy and hard, but so worth it.

As I said, this season was terrifying for me. My tool—breaking agreements and worshiping Jesus no matter what—simply wasn't adequate anymore. I knew Jesus, and I loved Him so much, but it felt like the floor of my soul was caving in. Would He help me? Why wasn't it enough to know His love and trust Him?

There was a gift in this season, but I didn't know it. Jesus wanted to take me beyond "swatting flies" to heal the wound that was drawing them. I didn't know this, but He did. I needed to come to the end of my rope and become willing to take the next hard step.

My husband Brian loves to renovate and has given me many tangible examples of what this process looks like. He finds joy in taking something old and broken and restoring it to full function, like my writing desk. He doesn't like to throw stuff out. This is one of the ways in which he reflects the image of his Creator.

I also know it can be so much work.

He recently renovated a house that had been lived in by renters for more than twenty years. The linoleum was old and full of holes. The plush carpet was a horror of hidden filth. The ceiling was coated in decades of cooking grease and nicotine stains. It was ugly and smelled to high heaven.

Brian and the owner saw the potential for what could be and were willing to pay the price.

The first step of renovation is an absolute mess. Everything gets torn up and pulled out. The stuff that gets uncovered can be shocking and repulsive. Every renovation uncovers more than what was originally bargained for, as well as flaws in the original construction. Without a vision for what it could be, it would be so much easier just to torch the whole thing.

Renovation initially looks like destruction. How can we know it's not? Simply by putting the whole mess in the hands of the Great Renovator. He loves restoring broken things and is really gentle. This is a radical act of surrender and I believe He takes that trust as a gift.

I love to check in on my husband's projects. Once the rubble is cleared, amazing things happen. New paint. New doors. New cabinets. Tiles. Flooring. As a project goes on, the excitement increases because you know it's going to be so beautiful. The hardest part is deciding if it's going to be worth the work.

THE TOOL

Count the cost. What's the long-term cost of hiding the "rotting floor" under the linoleum for just a little longer, or at least as long as possible?

HERE'S HOPE

The one who created you is the one who can restore you. None of this is a surprise to Him. He has a plan. He has resources. He has strategies. He is gentle.

There's absolutely nothing He wants more than to make your life flourish again. You are deeply loved.

HEALTHY LAMENT

Chapter Eleven

A lament or lamentation is a passionate expression of grief...[10]
—Wikipedia

Lament: Straight talk with God about the bad job he's doing...
at least from your perspective.[11]
—Urban Dictionary

IN MY ENTHUSIASM OVER THE EFFECTIVENESS OF BREAKING
agreements with lies and declaring truth, I used it all the time for everything. I loved the freedom and joy that came with living aligned with truth.

I was also terrified of sinking back into depression. I could not and
would not tolerate a negative thought or feeling very long. Worship and
praise and thanksgiving were my daily habits, and they were very good
ones. I highly recommend them.

Despite all this, I still had days when tears flowed out of control and I
despaired of ever getting over this, whatever "this" was. I didn't know. I was
confused, afraid, and probably a little ashamed. What would people think
if they knew of my private but uncontrolled weeping? What if I got to the
point where I couldn't keep it private any longer? Was I losing my mind?
How could this be when I was trying so hard to live and walk in truth?

It's ineffective to use the right tool for the wrong job. I was using what
was meant to be a weapon of warfare against the lies of the enemy of my
soul as a way to suppress pain. Used wrongly, it became a form of denial.

Denial is a poor choice. It leads to toilets falling through the floor.

I feel confident that Jesus was delighted at my attempts to use this
tool, but He is so gracious that He constantly wants to give us upgrades.

It was time for me to get an upgrade. I needed to learn how to process the sad, negative, ugly things and not get stuck in them. I needed to learn how to process in a healthy way.

I once heard a great analogy about emotions: they're like kids in a car. You can't throw them in the trunk, but you can't let them drive the car either. They're telling you something important and you need to listen to them, but keep them in their place.

You have emotions by design. If you're a highly analytical person you might be more inclined to call your feelings "thoughts," but they are still sourced in emotion.

Not everyone's emotional spectrum is the same in terms of intensity of highs and lows, but we are all designed with these dashboard indicators. They tell us important things about what we're thinking and experiencing.

We experience emotions as surprise, joy, sadness, anger, disgust, fear, shame, etc., and some of us know each of these in at least a dozen different shades. A healthy person experiences a full spectrum of emotion and recognizes the value and purpose of these feelings. Each sends an important message that we need to decode.

However, we have learned that not all emotions are safe. In fact, some are downright uncomfortable. We don't know what to do with others. We've been trained in how to manage some and ignore others.

Some of you may think you have limited feelings or emotions. This may be because you stuffed them in the trunk a long time ago and threw away the key. Some of you let your feelings drive the car and it's a disaster for you and everyone around you.

In this helpless season, I was trying to stuff my dark feelings in the trunk so I could get on with my life, but they kept sneaking out and tackling me. It was driving me nuts! Jesus was ready and waiting to teach me a new strategy.

I needed to listen to what my feelings were telling me and learn to process them in a healthy way. Stuffing down your emotions simply leads to a constipated heart. Just as you release gas when your physical body is constipated, your soul releases "gas" when your heart is blocked up with stifled and unresolved pain. This can manifest as outbursts of anger, weeping, irritability, and accusation. It's definitely uncomfortable, sometimes embarrassing, and generally unpleasant for everyone around you.

The only cure is to have a good emotional poop. How does one do this without getting trapped in the outhouse? We all know people who live there and it's not pretty.

Those closest to us tend to suffer the most. I was truly distressed when I lost my temper with my kids and when I had nothing to offer my husband but a tearful mess. I was ashamed of the ways I sometimes responded to people outside my home. Internally I blamed everyone around me. If they would only behave differently, my life would be easier. I would feel loved and safe, I would be calmer, and everything would generally be better. I didn't know that this relentless accusation was simply another strategy of the enemy of my soul.

While those around us definitely have an impact on us, we don't have to be a victim of their behaviour. This involves demonstrating self-control and setting boundaries in the way we respond.

Little did I know, most of my reactions were a result of others bumping into the wounds of my soul, sending shockwaves through me. Jesus wanted to heal those wounds. The next step in my renovation was to face them squarely. I was so afraid of going there, since I had been there before. Sorrow left unresolved does lead to depression. I had lived around major depression in my extended family my whole life and I sure didn't want my kids growing up in that atmosphere.

So how do we do this? I learned from the psalms. Some have accused King David of being manic depressive. I think he was just on to something and I'm so thankful it's been preserved for us.

David's pattern in many of the psalms goes like this: lament, remember what God has done, and worship. He didn't simply stuff down his pain; he poured it out to God. He didn't remain stuck there.

Having dumped out all his emotion, he brought his mind to bear on the situation. What did he know about God? What had God done for him and others in the past? What had God promised him? This brought comfort and hope to the situation and stirred up thanksgiving and praise.

Please note that you cannot skip ahead to the praise and thanksgiving part without thoroughly engaging in the first steps. This is what I had been doing and it wasn't healthy.

I want to be clear that I'm speaking specifically to the spiritual and emotional aspects of our being. It's important to realize that there are also physical symptoms that affect our emotions. The acronym HALT comes in handy as an easy checklist: are you hungry, angry, lonely, or tired? I also add hormonal! While this can help us become aware of what's going on under the surface, dealing with these emotions will clarify what's what.

Also, if you've struggled with depression for some time, it's important to talk to your doctor. There is a time and place for medication. Just don't stop there. Continue to care for your emotional and spiritual health.

Feeling overwhelmed or confused is one indicator that you might need to go into a time of lament. Taking the time to process your lament will help you unravel and sort things out. You will feel empowered to address your situation.

Over the years, I've refined this process. Are you ready, or at least curious?

What wound did Jesus show you when you asked Him about wounds from your past? What came to mind? Don't dismiss it if what came to mind doesn't seem like a big deal. Jesus is wise and kind. Remember my friend who was safely boring? When Jesus brought to her mind the experience of her not being chosen for the school play, her first reaction was to scoff. Those things happen to everyone! But I encouraged her to trust Jesus.

Often we need to tackle a "small" sorrow before we can think of looking at a big trauma. Jesus knows what string to pull to unravel everything. You might feel undone just by considering this, but I'm talking about unravelling the deadly and toxic things that have become reinforced in your soul. The essence of you will remain intact, held by Jesus.

You might also feel absolutely overwhelmed just thinking about doing this, quite certain that if you go there you'll fall apart beyond repair. I can reassure you that you won't. It will be messy, as renovation always is. Simply pick your space and time.

You might also ask a wise and mature friend to sit with you in this, but I would caution you against choosing someone who'll just want to rush in and fix things. It must be someone who trusts Jesus and is willing to wait through the process with you. Perhaps someone who has already read and successfully applied this book.

It takes so much courage to do this. Even though I've sat with countless people and coached them through this process, I still struggle to do it for myself sometimes. It just isn't fun to feel the hard stuff. It can uncover some ugly things. Yet it's worth it every single time. If you follow the process all the way through, it will lead you to a wide open space.

THE TOOL

Now that you know what Jesus is highlighting, the next step is to pour out your heart to God. He will help you (Psalm 62:8).

What happened that caused you pain, disappointment, fear, or loss? I would encourage you to write all of this down. Name it. Even if you aren't one to journal, take a piece of scrap paper and write bullet points or just words. *Do not edit.* Our grown-up brains have a way of explaining and excusing things. This is helpful in maturity, but not helpful in lamenting.

What happened? This is your own private lament. Don't worry about saying "bad things" about people you love. You aren't throwing anyone under the bus. What you're doing is uncovering the strategy of the enemy of your soul.

The next step is very important. How did this event or experience make you feel? You might have to be still or quiet for a few minutes to allow things to float to the surface. When we've locked our feelings in the trunk for a long time, they may not automatically pop out.

Give yourself permission to feel. There's a list of feeling words on page 141 that might help you get started. Ask Jesus to bring things to light and remember that He's holding you in this process. It won't destroy you. Rather, it will lead to healing.

Hang on to that scrap of paper. You're going to need it for the next few chapters.

HERE'S HOPE

Now that you've ripped off the bandage, the whole stinking mess is undeniable, but it's also ready to be cleansed and healed.

There are challenging steps ahead, but the worst part is over.

SAMPLE
LAMENT

Interlude

I AM INCLINED TO CALL THIS SECTION A "SUP-LAMENT," BECAUSE A little humour goes a long way for me when I'm dealing with pain.

I'll include a soundbite from one of David's laments, to give you permission to perhaps unlock your own heart. We all know those people who just cannot stop lamenting and need to learn to tighten it up a bit, but I know others who can hardly start. They just haven't learned how. Or worse, they've been taught that it's all kinds of wrong.

Over a third of the psalms recorded in the Bible are written as laments—outpourings of sorrow and frustration. King David of old, author of many of the psalms, was called a man after God's own heart, or a man whose heart *"beats with [God's] heart"* (Acts 13:22, MSG). David doesn't mince words one bit when he's on a roll, and I sometimes wonder whether even our most modern translations do justice to his passionate language. It's absolutely essential that we know how to do this. God can handle our pain; He has given us permission through David's example and even invites it.

It can be really helpful to find a psalm that echoes your heart and use it to give language to your own experience, especially if you haven't done this before.

Here's a sample that I have personally found helpful. Read it out loud. Try it on for size.

Turn to me and have mercy, for I am alone and in deep distress. My problems go from bad to worse. Oh, save me from them all! Feel my pain and see my trouble. Forgive all my sins. See how many enemies I have and how viciously they hate me! Protect me! Rescue my

life from them! Do not let me be disgraced, for in you I take refuge.
May integrity and honesty protect me, for I put my hope in you.
—Psalm 25:26–21

What is your response to those words? Do you feel them? Perhaps you feel a bit of disgust. This would be a clue that you've learned to put away weakness and guard against vulnerability. This is armour you'll have to lay aside in order to grow in spiritual and emotional health.

Read those verses again. Get curious. Wonder what is going on in David's life. Consider times when you may have had a similar response.

David's words blend petition with his anguish. He is raw and honest, and also desperate. In other psalms, he wonders aloud if God has abandoned him altogether. He calls out hellfire and damnation on his enemies.

When you lament, pretty much anything goes. Just pay attention. If you start to enjoy yourself, you're no longer lamenting—you're wallowing, having a pity party, or just being a jerk. Lamenting is about getting real with your pain, not simply complaining or crapping on people.

BANANA SEAT BIKES

Chapter Twelve

Everyone says that forgiveness is a lovely idea until they have something to forgive.[12]

—C.S. Lewis

WHEN I WAS NINE YEARS OLD, I TRIED TO TAKE MY BROTHER FOR A ride on the back of my banana seat bike. This is something my mother had emphatically told me not to do, but I was sure that I could pull it off and that she was just trying to wreck my fun. So I did it anyway.

Sound familiar? Like an event in an ancient garden?

We lived on an unpaved cul-de-sac. You're probably not as surprised as I was that this didn't turn out well.

It was all fun and games as I went ripping down the slope of our driveway, my five-year-old brother shrieking with delight on the seat behind me. However, as soon as I needed to make a turn, all was lost. We crashed and skidded across the gravel. Blood everywhere.

My poor baby brother ran wailing to the house where my mom met him at the door with wide open arms.

I don't think there was a speck of skin remaining on my left knee. There was, however, a lot of dirt and blood. I limped the bike back to the garage and I don't think I ever rode it again.

I skulked into the bathroom and did my best to clean up my knee. It was so painful. I could hardly bear to touch it. After wiping off most of the surface dirt, I slapped a bandage on it and went on my way. I was too ashamed to ask my mom for help. She was occupied with caring for the victim of my crime and understandably very annoyed with me.

To this day, I have several scars on that knee. Little bits of gravel remain there as a visual reminder that you should probably listen to your mom. It doesn't hurt anymore. Over time my body produced tough skin to isolate the dirt and keep it from poisoning the rest of my body.

So it is with our souls—there is dirt in our wounds. Most of us grow up with a few callouses wrapped around rocks that we simply didn't know how to deal with any other way. Those callouses make us feel safe, but they're actually dead spots that keep us from connecting well and experiencing a full and dynamic life. While we're often able to survive with that dirt stuck in there, we constantly fight infection or simply live with a dead spot. It's fine. We're fine. We'll be okay. Look at us, surviving!

But we were made for so much more than fine. We have been designed to thrive and flourish, not merely survive. And we have a Healer who made a way for restoration. He created us. We are precious to Him. He wants to clean the junk out of the wounds in our souls.

Some of you don't think you are worthy of His healing attention. After all, He told you not to ride the bike and you did anyway. You did the best you could to clean out the wound yourself and you would rather not give it any more attention. Some of you may feel like the victim of someone else's defiance in taking the bike out for a spin. You may not be sure you want to let that badge go.

There's a trap at either end of the spectrum, with a whole host of other filthy bits in between. Fear, shame, rejection, insignificance, rebellion, anger, bitterness, hopelessness, performance, and self-pity are just a few of the rocks commonly stuck in old wounds.

Wherever there's infection, we are drained of vitality and energy. We constantly try to cope and compensate. Where callous has built up on the soul, we are deprived of deep and meaningful relationships. Our capacity to experience true joy is limited to the extent that we've shut off pain. Creativity and expression are stunted by the deadness.

All of this robs us and the world around us of the powerful flourishing that happens when we show up as we were originally created, restored to a fuller expression of glory.

The first step in removing the bits is forgiving those who caused the pain in the first place. It might be someone else, or it might be yourself. As you poured out your heart in lament, who were the principal characters in the story? They are often authority figures or people with whom we have close relationships.

Forgiveness is key to healing and it's really, really hard. Sometimes we don't want to admit that someone else has hurt us—it's humbling and vulnerable. Sometimes we think we're protecting ourselves by hanging on to our pain.

I once sat with a guy who was in a paramilitary organization. He had been terribly betrayed by someone and it had cost him and his family a lot. He struggled so hard with this step that he broke into a sweat. This big, fit guy who was built for battle was facing one of the toughest challenges of his life. He said he would rather go beat someone up than forgive this person. That would have felt really good in the moment, but it wouldn't have brought healing. This old wound began to infect his marriage and his parenting.

He was fighting for freedom and the battle would be absolutely worth it, but it wouldn't be easy.

It's important to have a proper understanding of forgiveness. Forgiveness is not saying that what was done is okay, that it doesn't matter, or that we're just letting it go. It is a fierce act of courage and faith.

When we forgive someone, we're choosing to give all the loss they caused to Jesus for Him to redeem. Jesus didn't simply take the cost of your sins on Himself; He also took the cost of the sins of others to the cross. That is, He is willing to pay the price for their sin against you. Even when others are sorry, it cannot always repair the damage. Only Jesus can fully do that.

When we forgive others, we're basically taking the bill for the damages others have caused us and handing it to Jesus for Him to pay.

Forgiving someone doesn't magically remove the consequences of their actions. Nor does receiving grace for your own failures remove the consequences of your actions. Rather, the extending and receiving of grace *makes space* for something profoundly beautiful to emerge from the mess. Jesus will walk with you through the aftermath and make something whole out of it.

This isn't a way to simply wave a magic wand at our very real losses; it's a way to acknowledge that there's something and Someone who trumps the facts of our broken stories. Pain, loss, betrayal, and disappointment don't have to be the last word on your life.

When you look at your lament, it's probably pretty obvious who you need to forgive, yet it's a good idea to ask Jesus if you need to add anyone to the list. It's quite common for a name to pop up that wasn't immediately obvious.

Perhaps you feel concerned that this is getting way too introspective, and let me reassure you that it's not! I'm not recommending navel-gazing. That will just give you a really stiff neck and indigestion. I'm urging you to look up to Jesus in a posture of hope. He is the engineer of your healing and He knows exactly what you need.

The enemy of your soul would love nothing more than to brush something significant under the rug, because he loves to see you tormented. Jesus is wise and passionate about your wholeness. Trust Him in the process.

When I teach this at retreats, I make space for activation at the end of every session. A few years ago at a ladies retreat, I got to this step and invited participants to ask Jesus who He would like them to forgive. There was a woman present who had come with a truckload of pain. Her head said that she should start with forgiving her wretched unfaithful husband. However, when she asked Jesus, her mother's name kept rising up in her heart. She thought that was silly, because her mom was probably the least of her problems at that point, but it kept coming to her.

So she trusted the process and went with what she thought Jesus was saying, asking Him what it was that she needed to forgive. Immediately it came to her that she needed to forgive her mom for making them move when she was thirteen.

Again, her brain fought with her heart. That was silly. It's just part of life that people need to move, and sometimes for really good reasons. However, she chose to engage in the steps I'm about to lay out.

I'll never forget the transformation I saw take place in this brave woman. Tears came, not in great heaving sobs but in a steady, gentle, cleansing stream. She wept as she walked through each step, surprised by what she discovered. Her thirteen-year-old heart, which had experienced profound loneliness and a deep sense of abandonment, encountered Jesus in a beautiful, powerful, healing way.

I had noticed her immediately at the beginning of the retreat because she was physically a very beautiful woman while also looking absolutely beaten down. When she finished this process, she was positively radiant.

The best part of this story, if there is any one part that could be considered more wonderful than another, is that she rarely communicated with her mom. They weren't close, but they were "fine." As we wrapped up for a lunch break, she checked her phone, paused, and started weeping and laughing all at the same time. Her mother had sent her a text which included a photo of her as a baby and a message about how her mom had felt about her when she was born. She couldn't remember a time when her mother had spoken such words of blessing over her.

These words released a whole new level of healing. Her soul was being cleansed and healed before our very eyes. It was a moment of such holy wonder and unfettered joy. Every woman present encountered Jesus in that moment. In some mysterious way, the daughter forgiving her mother had also released the mother into freedom.

Why did she need to forgive her mother first? Jesus knew. The healing she had experienced in this process was essential for the hard work that was ahead in her marriage. The pain in her marriage was that much more excruciating because it was pressing on this old wound that was hardly even noticeable to her anymore in light of more recent pain. Yet this healing encounter provided the resilience she needed to engage in the process ahead.

I saw her a year later. She was still radiant and held her head high. She was also still married. And though it wasn't easy, she had lots of hope that they were making progress in the right direction.

Trust Jesus. He created you and knows what you need. He is both fierce and tender over you.

THE TOOL

If you've written out your lament, circle the names of the key players. This could include yourself and God. Otherwise, simply note the names of those who have come to mind as you read this chapter.

HERE'S HOPE

As you engage in the process, you're going to experience unexpected restoration. Right now, receive an expectation of goodness without forming an agenda of what that might look like.

If you're feeling impatient with this process and just want to get on with it, I encourage you to take a deep breath. We will get there!

I want you to be well informed and have a deep understanding of the process in which you are engaged. It has been my experience that this will have a deep and long-lasting impact. With a deeper understanding, you will be able to take ownership and engage powerfully rather than passively.

All these tools are assembled step by step for easy reference at the end of the book.

COSMIC COURTROOM

Each time we are injured, we stand at the same fork in the road and choose to travel either the path of forgiveness or the path of retaliation.[13]

—Desmond Tutu

I BELIEVE THERE'S AN EPIC BATTLE GOING ON OVER THIS PROCESS OF forgiveness. Jesus clearly told us that if we don't forgive, the inevitable fall-out is torment (Matthew 18:21–35). The enemy of your soul lives for your torment.

If it seems like I'm belabouring this point of forgiveness, I do not apologize. I'm constantly surprised by people who fail to recognize the power they have by resisting this step. Or by how they simply fail to recognize the need for it. They're fine.

Except obviously they aren't. It's not that I lack compassion for the depth of pain people have experienced, but I'm so passionate about freedom. I know from firsthand experience the power of forgiveness. It is hard but very powerful and totally worth the painful work of the process.

If you haven't caught on yet, I'm a very visual person. Stories help me understand things in a deep and meaningful way. Scripture gives us many metaphors and pictures to help us understand what's going on behind the scenes in our stories.

The following illustration always helps me lean into the process of forgiveness.

I want you to picture a royal court, a large hall thronging with people. At one end sits God the Father. He is not cold, angry, or indifferent. He is alert to all that is happening. He is keenly aware that many people in the room are suffering and is committed to bringing justice to each one. He's like the best father you've ever met. Then multiply that exponentially. You cannot overestimate His goodness (Psalm 46:5–9, 89:14, Jeremiah 8:21, Luke 15:11–31).

Jesus is right there beside the Father. He has scars on His forehead, side, hands, and feet. He's somehow both perfectly at ease and poised for action. His eyes blaze with fire that is equal parts mercy and truth. It's almost hard to look Him in the eye, but if you do, His gaze will rip through you like a blast of fresh air that clarifies, awakens, and makes you almost giddy, as though you've inhaled pure oxygen. It will make you weak in the knees and stronger than you have ever been. You will see that He's not afraid. Hope will begin to stir in you (Revelation 19:12, John 20:27, Psalm 85:10, 2 Corinthians 12:8–10).

To your right is the accuser. He stands there day and night, hurling accusations. A stream of words flows continuously from his mouth, naming facts and colouring them with lies. His minions shout and cheer from time to time, repeating his words. Sometimes others in the court cheer and chant an echo. The noise can become deafening, even crushing (Revelation 12:10–17).

Where are you in this court? Are you ready to plead your case? Have you already been shouting with fist raised, cursing and demanding justice? Perhaps you're hiding in the back corner, not sure if your case is worthy of attention. Either way, your name has been called and it's time to present your case.

In the presence of the good Father, you are invited to tell your story and name what has been lost, stolen, or destroyed. He wants to hear what you have to say. He thinks it matters. He has time for you.

Picture your offender in the accused's box. It may be someone else or even yourself. What did they do? What has it cost you? Pour out your heart. Hold nothing back.

Of course, the accuser is clamouring. He has so much to say. It's your fault! It's his fault! It's her fault! It's God's fault! Blame, blame, blame. Hurling mud and hoping something sticks. Some of what he says feels really true and something inside you wants to jump up beside him and point the finger and yell along, unleashing all your bitter fury on your offender.

The facts are on the table. Wrong has been done. It is undeniable. There has been loss. The desire for punishment is so strong you can taste it. It feels as though retribution will set something to rights.

Now what?

Jesus steps forward with His eyes full of fierce compassion. He's nodding, not for a minute denying the facts of the case. He has walked in your shoes and knows the agony of injustice and it's not okay with Him. He is fully invested in your case. He asks if you're willing to release the offender to Him to deal with. He would like to pay your offender's debt to you— not just what is owed, but double what is owed (Zechariah 9:11–12). He would like to make something beautiful out of the mess on your hands.

What are you going to do?

You could join the accuser and just stay there a little longer, venting and shouting. It will feel good. Eventually it will consume you. Twist you. Warp you.

You could walk away in disgust and blend into the crowd of people wallowing in their loss and disappointment. You can carry on a little longer, clutching your broken bits and saying you're fine. Perhaps you have a group of supporters in the room with similar stories. They give you a sense of belonging. Who will you be if you give up membership? There is risk in giving up the things that have defined you.

You could accept the offer of Jesus. Do you trust Him? He is offering to pay the debt owed to you and deal with the injustice. It will be in His time and His way (Isaiah 30:18, Romans 12:19). A lot of surrender is involved. He is not pushy at all, but He is intense in His desire to help you. You get to choose.

If you take Jesus up on His offer, you have an advocate ready to take things from there. Jesus promised to send this advocate to offer comfort, counsel, encouragement, and help. This advocate is His Holy Spirit. He will constantly remind you that you are a deeply loved child of God as you walk along in your restoration journey. The Spirit will refresh your faith and restore hope. The Spirit will help you sort out what part of the mess is yours to clean up. He will bring wisdom in what to say and when. He will bring a sweet, clean conviction that helps you know how to do life differently going forward. The Spirit will sustain your joy while you wait for every promise of God to be fulfilled.

This court is a place for you to deal with the fallout of things that have been all kinds of wrong in your life. It's a place to acknowledge those unseen players in your story and an opportunity to call out the work of the destroyer and align yourself with your Creator and His strategies to restore everything.

This spiritual court doesn't replace the due process of natural laws. Where laws have been broken, there are consequences. Those who have broken laws and harmed others must be dealt with in a way that prevents them from doing further damage. If there's something you need to report to an authority, please do not remain silent.

THE TOOL

It's time to rumble. What will you do? This is an act of your will, a choice you will make. It's not a feeling.

If you are experiencing internal resistance, it may simply be the protest of the enemy of your soul resisting the loss of his influence in your life. Break agreement with rebellion. Be fierce about freedom.

HERE'S HOPE

There was once a man who came to Jesus quite timidly. His son was tormented, experiencing terrible convulsions that regularly threatened to kill him. The father was understandably desperate and came to Jesus asking for mercy, to help if He could.

"What do you mean, 'If I can'?" Jesus asked. "Anything is possible if a person believes."
The father instantly cried out, "I do believe, but help me overcome my unbelief!"
—Mark 9:23–24

It was enough. The boy was healed.

Perhaps you come to this scenario not quite sure if you dare let go and trust Jesus. I love this story so much because it reassures me that if all I can do is say "I believe, but help me overcome my unbelief," it is enough.

He will meet you with your little seed of faith and match it with extravagant goodness.

ROCK
PICKING

Chapter Fourteen

You will have to meet your pain and speak its name.[14]

—Desmond Tutu

WHEN I HAD MY EPIC BANANA SEAT BIKE WIPEOUT, ROCKS BECAME embedded in my knee. I wish I had let my mom help me clean out the wound properly, but shame kept me from asking. I did the best I could on my own, but I didn't do a very good job. Probing a wound is incredibly painful. I remember gasping, tears rising, ringing in my ears. It seemed easier to cover it with a bandage and hope for the best.

As you bravely take this next step, you will feel pain. Tears may rise and chances are you may want to quit. Don't try to do it on your own. Invite your advocate, the Holy Spirit, to help you. Take deep breaths. Lock eyes with Him. Let Him hold you and direct you in this process. It will be worth it.

Reflect on your lament. What are the actions that caused the loss in your life? What was the result? Naming these things will bring clarity and focus to your healing process.

Jesus told His followers to forgive from the heart, not just go through the motions (Matthew 18:35). I don't think this means we have to feel like forgiving. Rather, we need to allow our hearts to engage in the process— to feel, to go below the surface of the actions to understand their impact on our hearts.

We have to let those feelings out of the trunk so we can deal with them. This may be harder for some than others. For some, this may be more of an analytical process than an emotional one. Trust Jesus to meet you there. Ask Him to bring up the things He wants you to address. He is willing and able to guide you through every step.

Forgiving from the heart actually means acknowledging, naming, or feeling the loss rather than covering it with anger. It isn't enough to simply say, "I forgive Bob for being a jerk." While that can be satisfying, the satisfaction lies in accusation and venting frustration. It's more effective to unpack the loss: "I forgive Bob for lying about me and costing me a promotion. It made me feel angry, powerless, and hopeless." The more we get into what is really going on inside us, the more effectively we cleanse the wound.

For years I forgave people rather robotically, simply saying things like, "I forgive Mike." This seemed to check the box. I'd feel like I had done the right thing, but it sure wasn't effective.

People would tell me that sometimes you just have to forgive the same person over and over until you no longer twitch over that event. While there is some truth in that, I've learned that forgiving people from the heart—going deeper into what's really going on—is far more effective. When I take that approach, I've found myself able to move on much more quickly into a place of honestly being okay. Sometimes I do still need to forgive a second or third time, but through that process I usually discover things I wasn't quite aware of the first time.

Once you have named the actions, what they brought into your life, and how they've caused you to feel, consider the mess.

I find it helpful to attach a visual image to this. A bucket of shattered glass. A heap of broken toys. A mess of bloody bandages. Your own battered heart. What do your pain and loss look like? Whatever it looks like for you, this is what you're going to give to Jesus.

There is a powerful act of surrender in this step. Will you give this to Jesus and put your hope in Him for full restoration? He won't leave you empty-handed, but your hands must be emptied to receive what He has for you.

When we forgive someone from the heart, we release them from any *obligation* to make things right with us. This doesn't mean that we let them off the hook and it doesn't mean there won't be any consequences for what they've done. We're simply saying that they don't need to pay us what is owed in order for us to be okay, because we're giving their debt to Jesus. It's between Him and them to settle that. Justice is in His hands, not ours.

It's also important to remember that this is not about reconciliation. Reconciliation involves both parties. Forgiveness is something we can participate in even if our offender is dead, not the least bit repentant, or not even slightly apologetic.

Unfortunately, brokenness can have a cascading effect. When others harm or offend us, we tend to respond in broken ways. We tend to attach judgments to their behaviour. This usually feels good, but it traps and hinders us. It definitely reinforces the rift in the relationship.

There's a difference between acknowledging facts and making judgments. For example, it may be a fact that Kathy never talks to me. But we may move into judgment by attaching a motive to the fact: "Kathy never talks to me because she's a snob who doesn't care about anyone." This is making a judgment. We may be right. We're probably wrong. Only God knows what is in a person's heart.

Either way, if we judge others, we will receive the same judgment. We effectively curse others with these judgments and become bound up in the process. In order to free ourselves, we need to revoke these judgments (Matthew 7:1–5, Romans 2:1–3).

Finally, Jesus taught His followers to forgive and even bless those who have wronged them—this is the pathway to freedom (Matthew 5:43–45). While unjustly imprisoned, the Apostle Paul taught, "*Bless those who persecute you. Don't curse them; pray that God will bless them… Don't let evil conquer you…*" (Romans 12:14, 21) This is an invitation to the high road! Not only are we going to release them of their debt, but we'll choose to lavish on them that which they least seem to deserve.

In our humanity, we often want to bless people with fix-it blessings. "I bless her with the ability to hold her tongue." "I bless him with the wisdom not to be a jerk." This can indicate that we haven't fully released the offender to Jesus for Him to deal with.

I encourage people to bless their offender with the thing they least deserve, or that which their offender would really, really like to have. I start by blessing them with knowing that they're deeply loved. Even if everyone around them thinks they're a total jerk, God does indeed love them and it is His love that will lead them to live in a new and different way. Love is something we all need.

Another blessing that can never go wrong is to bless your offender to flourish in their life, finances, and relationships. I know it's counterintuitive, but we overcome evil with good! (Romans 12:20)

I see blessing as a radical act of war against bitterness. Blessing someone who has wronged you is the absolute antithesis of victimhood. As Paul said, it is a refusal to let evil conquer you.

In fact, I like to get carried away with this step. The more I can engage with blessing, the more I feel like I'm taking back parts of my own soul that have been lost. Choosing to bless also helps me to walk forward in the freedom of forgiveness.

Not surprisingly, as I write this I'm working through a situation in my own life. Something pierces my heart almost every day with a fresh reminder of what I've lost. I have done the hard work of lament and processed forgiveness and had many necessary conversations, yet I'm living with a level of loss.

I'm not at the end of this particular chapter in my story. Every time it comes up, I bless the people who hurt me. This actively keeps bitterness at bay and keeps me from becoming overwhelmed by the sense that I'm a victim of their behaviour. In the process of blessing, I remember the grace and goodness of God and feel encouraged and revived.

Sometimes the person you need to forgive is yourself. You may be keenly aware that you made poor choices. You didn't listen and rode the bike anyway. This has led to regret and loss and you feel like you deserve all the consequences you're experiencing.

Through this process, you are binding yourself in bitterness and judgment. Until you deal with that, you will never be free. Perhaps you believe that by hanging on to this condemnation you are preventing yourself from doing stupid things in the future. This simply isn't true. This will hold you in bondage to the past.

Receive grace—that is, accept the truth that Jesus has mercy and compassion toward you and would like to help you clean up the mess you've made. He is so extravagant in His kindness. Not only did He take your punishment, but He promises to help you clean up your mess and even make something beautiful out of it. He wants to free you to move forward in a healthy life in which you are able to flourish.

Sometimes the one you need to "forgive" is God. Perhaps a more accurate way to express this is to say that you renounce the accusations you've made against Him. When things go horribly sideways, we often feel like God has abandoned us or should have stopped things from happening in the first place. We accuse God of not doing what we think He should have done. We cannot receive the healing love we need from Him when we're holding Him in judgment.

Forgiveness must become a lifestyle, since there are endless opportunities for offence. We live in a world of broken people, and because our own brokenness can leave us feeling touchy, we need to revisit forgiveness often. If you find yourself getting irritable with someone, check to see if there's something you need to forgive.[15] You may need to have a conversation with this person, but the conversation will go much better if you get the rocks out of your soul first.

Feeling offended is definitely an indication that you need to forgive. The really good news is that it becomes easier, or at least more natural, with practice! Freedom is also addictive.

Are you ready to put this into practice? You might want to try this with a smaller rock before taking on the boulders in your soul. That's okay. It will build resilience for the process.

As I write this, I'm praying for you, dear reader. I ask the Holy Spirit of God to infuse you with strength as you make this courageous move. I pray that He will fill you with His comfort and wisdom and direct you through each step.

THE TOOL

Use the following template and adapt it to your story. You can use your own words, but I encourage you to make sure you incorporate each step. It's not a magic formula, but it does cover the important principles in the process.

Take the paper with your lament and use it to fill in the prompts. It's incredibly helpful to say these words out loud. When you do this, you're engaging your whole being—spirit, soul, and body. Begin by thanking God for His love. This humble acknowledgement of your own need sets a good posture.

Thank You, God, for Your love. As an act of my will, I choose to forgive (offender) for (name their actions). This made me feel (name the cost and feelings: afraid, unable to trust, abandoned, ashamed, insignificant, hopeless, rejected, etc.). It caused (name any fallout in your life). I give all of this pain and loss to You, Jesus, and I put all my hope in You to restore everything that has been lost and broken. I now release (offender) from any obligation to make things right with me and I release them from the judgments I have made. I bless them with (knowing they are deeply loved, etc.).

Saying this may have been hard, but doesn't it feel good? There is a quiet in your soul. A clarity in your mind. A sense that you can breathe more deeply. This is freedom.

You may need to spend quite a bit of time in this chapter. The first time we engage with this step, the list of people we need to forgive can be long. Do what you can and then take a break... but come back to it. Your life is too precious to leave in a state of toxicity.

HERE'S HOPE

In taking this difficult but courageous step, you have:

- been released from torment.
- gone from victim to victorious.
- taken the last word from your offender and given it to Jesus.
- changed your future.
- made space for healing that is spiritual, emotional, and often even physical.
- positioned yourself for a significant breakthrough in your healing journey.

Eradicating Infection

Chapter Fifteen

Cares and deception don't storm in; they sneak in.[16]

—Jon Tyson

WHEN YOU HAVE ROCKS IN A WOUND, IT'S A NO-BRAINER TO REMOVE the ones you can see. You might miss one or two and have to come back to them, but it just makes sense to remove the larger ones.

Yet there's something even more insidious than those rocks—the unseen bits of corruption that enter the wounds of our souls. Picture your soul having a naturally protective barrier, like your physical skin, and then picture events like trauma, betrayal, and disappointment piercing that healthy barrier. As adults, we remember the events, people, and words that define our story. These are the rocks. However, they are carriers of invisible critters that invade our soul and create infection.

Look back at the words in your forgiveness process. How did the actions of your offender make you feel?

Some readers may have a long list of feelings. Others may find that the only word they can come up with is "angry," which is totally legit. Be curious about that word. Why do you feel angry?

Anger is a secondary emotion. It's one we pick up to protect ourselves. We use it to make people back down and not hurt us further. Underneath anger, there are always other feelings. Sometimes it's bitterness and a desire to control or punish the offender, in which case leaning into the process of forgiveness will help to disarm anger.

Usually there is also fear attached to the anger. Dare to consider what you might be afraid of. If you've been using the armour of anger for as long as you can remember, it may take a while to sort out what else is going on. Be still and wait. Ask God to show you. Again, there is a list of feeling words on page 141 that might help to prime the pump.

Over my years of working with people, as well as living my own story, I have come to the conclusion that there is always a theme or pattern to the enemy's strategy in a person's life. A strategy is a plan of action designed to achieve a long-term goal. We go stumbling along through life's challenges unable to see the forest for the trees, but the enemy of your soul has one goal: to destroy the beauty and force of our original design.

The strategy of the enemy against us is in direct opposition to the destiny and purpose for which we were created. When we're oblivious to his strategy, his plan of action, we play into his hands. However, when we identify the strategy we can respond in a powerful way that undermines his grip on us.

When you use the forgiveness tool in the previous chapter, you'll begin to notice themes—specifically, where you identified your own answers to the "It made me feel…" prompt. This process is most effective when we don't let our rational brain try to edit these words too much. What we experience on a visceral level isn't always immediately logical. Being honest about what we're experiencing will help us pick up on the theme that reveals the enemy's strategy.

One of the major themes in my life has been a sense of abandonment. All humans have rejection in their story in some form. The enemy has lots of material to work with and his lies become very believable. The truth is that we're all deeply loved by our Creator and designed to function best when we're living from that love.

Whenever I've processed forgiveness for someone significant in my life, I've noticed the pain show up, among other words, such as "abandoned." This is what I felt or experienced in each scenario.

I got curious about this. I have loving parents and grew up in a relatively stable environment. It wasn't immediately logical to me that a deep sense of abandonment should define me. However, the enemy of our souls is sneaky. After all, if you're trying to get someone to believe a lie, you won't take the most obvious approach.

Trying to rationalize at such times is rarely helpful—remember, navel-gazing just gives you a stiff neck and indigestion. It's a really good idea to ask the advocate, the Holy Spirit, to reveal the root of these feelings. The Spirit has been watching over you and your destiny since long before you even knew you had one, waiting for the moment when you would exercise your powerful will to invite Him into your story. He has things He wants to show you in order to unlock freedom and launch you forward in your destiny.

For me, memories long forgotten began to bubble to the surface. I remembered significant people struggling with depression which made them emotionally absent. I remembered feeling overwhelmed by the grief, loss, and brokenness in our extended family. As a little girl, I recalled standing by as my family's attention and energy went into caring for my special needs brother.

These are human experiences. No one was doing anything intentionally malicious. I, too, have experienced depression that has affected my loved ones and have nothing but compassion for anyone struggling to do their best through that fog. Yet I acknowledge that these common experiences were the crack in the door that allowed a seed to settle into my soul. The enemy is a jerk and will take what he can get.

I want to pause here and look every reader in the eye. Resist shame and receive grace. You, your parents, and your children (if you have them) were born into a world at war. Sometimes we do epically stupid stuff and need to address that. Sometimes we do the best we can and still the enemy is there to rob us and our families. Recognize that at the root of every pain and loss is the work of the enemy. Definitely forgive those who partnered with his processes, either intentionally or unintentionally, but don't let either shame or accusation pin you down at this point. We all need grace, both given and received.

Our childhood experiences can have a snowball effect on us later in life. I hungered for attention, which led to a clinging desperation in my relationships. I was extra sensitive to rejection. If my husband was shut down or introspective, I felt disproportionate levels of anguish. I struggled with shyness, shame, and anxiety. Every instance of loneliness or rejection caused my soul to wither and further twist in on itself.

How did I cope with this pain? I shut down and withdrew. I was protecting a hurting little girl, but at the same time perpetuating a cycle.

Now, in my adulthood, those I loved were experiencing the same emotional abandonment that had launched me on this broken road. I can imagine the enemy crowing in delight as I got swept up in this pain-perpetuating cycle.

I was created for deep and meaningful relationship. So are you. I was particularly designed to be a messenger and communicator of God's healing love, but that design was thwarted when I was shut down and withdrawn. Without engaging in this hard work of renovation, I would remain part of a cycle of brokenness. When I finally recognized this strategy for what it was, I became fierce. Someone was going to have to break the cycle and I wanted it to be me!

In order to unravel the power of the lie, I had to forgive each person who had knowingly or unknowingly communicated this message of abandonment to me. The process of forgiveness isn't about accusing anyone or throwing them under the bus. It's simply how we uncover and disarm the strategy being used against us!

The next step was to identify the infection that had set in. My soul had embraced the lie that I was abandoned. My experiences weren't imaginary—they were plenty real—and the conclusions I had attached to these experiences were very logical, but they were not truth.

Through repeated experiences of emotional isolation, I had made an agreement with the lie that told me I was abandoned. It was as though we had shaken hands and nodded and agreed that we were in this together—I was emotionally abandoned and needed to be on guard against further abandonment.

What I really needed was to break up with this toxic lover. I needed to give the boot to all the rotten buddies of fear, shame, hopelessness, self-pity, and self-consciousness that abandonment had brought along. I also needed to learn how to live in a new way.

If you pause and consider three events in your life that have caused you pain or disappointment, you too will discover some overlap in the feelings caused by these events. Is there currently something really nagging at you because of the way a coworker, family member, or acquaintance behaved? Consider how that made you feel. Then ask yourself if this is something you also experienced as a child with one of your parents, your siblings, or a teacher? Is it something that often seems to define your life and relationships?

Hopefully, you're having an Aha! moment here. These common threads are clues about the infection that has set in your soul. These infections are constantly present, like a trigger waiting to be set off.

It doesn't have to always be this way. There is a way to deal with the infection.

This is when we need to pick up the breaking agreement tool, covered in Chapter Seven. By doing this, we go after the infection and make space for truth that will cleanse and heal the wound.

I cannot emphasize enough how important this is. We've all seen people who have gone through years of therapy but still have a chip on their shoulder. They can articulate their abuse and the effect it's had on them. They are vigilant and have much to say about how to stop cycles of abuse. There's a big difference between the effect of someone who recognizes pain and shouts about it and someone who has recognized pain and been healed. A chip on the shoulder can come across as a threat or warning—"If you trigger my pain, you'll be sorry." It may invite others to the riot, but it doesn't go a long way towards actually healing the wound. Healing is contagious and releases hope. It makes us both fierce and compassionate.

Healing begins with an *experience* of truth. For example, I could give mental assent to the truth that I haven't been abandoned because theologically I know that God says He will never leave me. This is good truth. However, our brain can give assent to something without our soul experiencing it. I knew this truth with my head but my heart wasn't living there because it had not *experienced* this truth. In fact, my strategy of withdrawal kept me from it!

When I broke agreement with the lie that I was abandoned, I asked Jesus to take it away and show me what He had for me instead. I waited in stillness and began to sense something thawing inside me. The hard scab of self-protection I had been using to shield my soul from this pain dissolved as I gave Him permission to take it away. Something new and different seeped into me and then filled me up. Washing over me. Unravelling me. What was this? Something like love but different.

It was delight. I was experiencing love in a fresh way, and it was healing. Jesus wasn't just telling me that He loved me, which my brain already knew. He was giving me a revelation of His delight in me. He didn't just like me, tolerate me, or love me because it is His nature to do so. He genuinely delighted in me!

This was so healing and empowering. If He delights in me, I could probably trust Him not to abandon me.

This was a total gamechanger. I was no longer just hanging on to truth with white knuckles. I had experienced something far beyond what my brain cells could grasp.

Jesus said I was delightful. This was truth my heart could sink roots into. This gave me something to live from when I bumped up against the brokenness of others.

All these years later, delight continues to define my life.

It isn't just true for me. It's true for you, too. When I teach this at workshops, I love getting the group to say it out loud: "I am delightful!" Usually it's a little pathetic on the first try. I get them to say it again. And then a third time. By then, their postures and facial expressions have changed. They're getting a taste of the sweetness and it is irresistible.

Try it for yourself. Right now say out loud, "I am delightful." Say it three times. Feel that? That's hope. Your body and brain are echoing what your heavenly Father has been declaring over you since long before you were born. When He dreamed of creating you, He was delighted. As you read this, your heavenly Father is shouting with joy over you. He's doing a happy dance as you begin to rise up against the strategies that have kept you from living loved (Zephaniah 3:17).

I have led countless people through this process and I can tell you that Jesus will speak to you in a way that is meaningful and personal. He can speak to you through any of your senses. You may simply experience warmth, comfort, or peace. You may have words of love or affirmation pop into your head. Perhaps a song. I've even had people get a whiff of a scent that speaks to them quite personally.

If nothing comes to you right away, don't freak out. This step definitely comes easier for some than others due to previous experiences, or even wiring. Simply say out loud, "Thank You, Jesus, for loving me. I receive Your love in the place of _____." This simple declaration will begin to undermine the stronghold of the enemy and make it easier for you to receive more. Jesus won't tell you that He is angry or condemn you. When we give Him our pain, He gives us healing.

There may be other things blocking your ability to receive, but we will get to that in future chapters. Simply know for now that you are loved. Say it out loud. Receive it. Breaking agreement is still having an effect. It is eroding the strategy of the enemy against you.

THE TOOL

Breaking agreement was introduced in an earlier chapter, but we're going to take it a step further now, applying it specifically to your forgiveness process to increase the level of restoration you experience. Saying these words out loud will put those spiritual forces of darkness on notice that you're done with their nonsense and help you take ownership over your being.

What feeling or experience words showed up when you processed forgiveness? Name those things in the tool below. Use the breaking agreement tool to tear up that contract and write a new one with the things Jesus is giving you.

In the name of Jesus, I break every agreement I have made with _____. I command _____ out of my thoughts and emotions, out of my actions and reactions, away from how I see myself and others, and away from my marriage and my children (if applicable). Jesus, I ask that You take this far away from me. What do You have for me instead?

HERE'S HOPE

When you break agreement, you aren't simply engaging in some flaky, feel-good activity. What you're doing is both physical and spiritual. You're actually affecting neural pathways in your brain.

Dr. Caroline Leaf is a neuroscientist whose work has helped me immensely on my journey. Her research indicates that every thought changes the chemistry of the brain. Thoughts produce chemicals that produce feelings and reactions. Thoughts are real things made of proteins that occupy physical space in our brains.[17]

When you break agreement, you cut off the fuel supply to cells that physically exist. When you receive fresh truth from Jesus, own it, and declare it, you're creating whole new pathways and releasing completely different chemicals into your body. This is a big deal!

UNFETTERED

Chapter Sixteen

I have wrapped my heart into yours all day long!

—Psalm 25:5, TPT

I USED TO HAVE THE SAME DREAM AT LEAST ONCE A YEAR IN WHICH three women from my past would prevent me from getting to something or someone. It could be something I wanted to do or somewhere I wanted to go. Or they might stop me from connecting with my husband.

It was the strangest thing. I didn't have any particularly strong feelings about these women and I had made sure to forgive each of them for the things I hadn't appreciated about our interactions. It was incredibly frustrating to me that the dreams continued. Why did these women continue to have this voice in my present?

I began to pick up on a theme in my pursuit of wholeness. Individuals and courses I attended would refer to "soul ties." I'm passionate about acknowledging the spiritual dimension of our lives and I'm also vigilant about not being flaky. Even though I thought this was a little sketchy, I leaned into learning more. It turns out that what I learned was incredibly helpful!

Most of us in North American culture have heard about attachment theory and codependency. These things give us clues about soul ties. Quantum physics indicates that we are all interconnected more than we realize. Quantum entanglement is a phenomenon wherein particles stay connected even though they're spatially separated. I can't claim to understand quantum physics, but I know there is enough science in it to suggest that maybe this concept of soul ties isn't totally nuts. If science and psychology point to a reality, I would bet any amount of money that there is also a spiritual dimension.

I have come to understand that we do indeed have a deeply spiritual connection to each other—a connection that can be either life-giving or harmful. For lack of a better word, I will refer to this connection as a soul tie.

We need to be bonded together. Secure attachment happens when a child has repeated experiences of feeling connected, understood, and protected.[18] Any time we experience a relationship that makes us feel seen, safe, and secure, we create a positive attachment. These healthy bonds are a gift from God. They are part of His design. Healthy attachment is an indication of a good soul tie.

In her classic work *Codependent No More*, Melody Beattie describes a codependent person as "one who has let another person's behaviour affect him or her, and who is obsessed with controlling that person's behaviour."[19] This is a great description of an unhealthy soul tie, though unhealthy soul ties can be so much more than codependency.

When we allow the words or actions of another person to define us apart from the truth of who God says we are, we form an unhealthy bond. When we demand connection or affirmation from someone which they cannot give, we place an unhealthy tie on them. Sexual experiences always create a bond, which can be positive or negative depending on the context. We can have unhealthy attachments to people who have passed away, abused us, or are no longer part of our lives, or even to places we treasured or where we experienced trauma. Any unhealthy tie can jerk us around, keep us from flourishing, and cause us to haemorrhage joy and emotional energy.

I was surprised to discover that our dreams can be great indicators of unhealthy soul ties. I immediately thought of my recurring dream of these three women. Many years later, it hardly seemed they should have a voice in my life.

One woman, Nora, had tried to play an uninvited maternal role in my life during my college years. I didn't especially like her, but she was an authority figure with a certain amount of influence. One day she pulled me aside to chat with me about my laugh. She told me that a young lady's laugh should sound more like a "rippling brook" than an explosion.

I'm sure she meant well. I'm equally sure that a phoney rippling brook laugh would have been revolting. I've laughed about this story many times over the years and my friends have reassured me that they definitely prefer my authentic laughter. If it sounds like an explosion, it's an explosion of joy.

It's interesting how many people have stories like this one. You know, the story your family loves to tell about you, or the one you tell that pokes a bit of fun at someone else. Every single time I dig into these stories I find that under the surface there remains a thread of pain. I can deny it, but through processing the story I realized it still has a pull on me. Nora's comment poked on a thread of insecurity that I was perhaps too much, too loud, too not-something-I-should-be.

The two other women in my dream were also people I knew from my college years. Though I hadn't had a particularly negative experience with them, I had really wanted their approval, believing that their affirmation would further my aspirations. I gave something of myself to each one. This was unhealthy because their voice carried greater weight than what God said was true about me.

After I broke my unhealthy ties with them, I never had one of those dreams again.

I have found this tool to be so helpful in a myriad of ways. I've met with people who were having unwanted dreams about former lovers, abusers, or even pornographic images—and once we dealt with the unhealthy tie, they ceased having these dreams.

When someone close to us dies, it's incredibly helpful to break the tie we share with them. Understandably, people are reluctant to do this. They loved this person. They feel like they will lose them altogether if they break ties. Yet these ties continue to drain their souls long after the loved one has passed.

Breaking ties with someone who has passed away isn't about getting over it or forgetting about them. Their assignment in your life is complete. It's no longer a life-giving relationship, though they may have left a wonderful legacy.

Breaking ties is even more imperative if their relationship with you was a destructive one. Whether your loss was a parent, friend, sibling, or child (including miscarried or aborted), I highly recommend that you use the tool I will share in just a few moments. You'll find that you are able to hold on to the sweetness of the memories without the bitterness of the loss.

Tim and Nicole have an ongoing struggle in their marriage. Nicole's primary love language is words of affirmation. Tim says he cannot express love to her that way. In the past, religious leaders had used affirming words to manipulate him and he feels that words have ceased to have meaning to him. Therefore, he won't use them with others.

While this may have a bit of a noble tone, the truth is that words are powerful. He is missing out on an amazing opportunity to love and encourage his wife. These religious leaders of his past have probably long forgotten him, but he has a bond with them that currently trumps the one he has with his wife.

The good news is that Nicole knows what to do with this pain. When she hears only negative, critical words and confronts her unmet longing for encouragement, she doesn't pretend that it doesn't hurt. She pours out her grief to God, forgives Tim, breaks agreement with the lies that tell her she isn't loved and cherished, and then breaks the unhealthy soul ties she's formed with Tim. She affirms her commitment to love him well and speaks a blessing over their marriage. Her roots are growing deep into God's love, making her a dangerous woman.

It will be a great day when Tim engages in his own healing process, but until then Nicole hasn't been left hanging; Jesus meets her in her place of need and her heart can remain tender.

James always dreamed of having his own farm. He finally achieved this dream but couldn't make it financially viable. After many years of hard work, he had to let it go in an auction to avoid bankruptcy.

You can imagine how painful this was for him and his family.

They moved far away for a job, and when James and his wife came back for a visit more than a year later I asked how they were doing. James said that he felt like his heart was still here with the farm and that he just hadn't been able to move on.

I asked him if we could walk through a process that might help. Because we're friends, he trusted me enough to try it. I led him through the process of forgiving himself for all the ways he felt he had failed. Then I got him to picture surrendering the land to God and I led him through breaking ties with the land.

A few weeks later, he sent me a text. He told me that he felt really free, full of joy, and was able to move on in his new life. What a beautiful thing! He and his wife are thriving in their new business.

We all have a mixture of healthy and unhealthy ties with our parents, children, and spouses. This is because these relationships are so significant! They are designed to be a gift, but every good gift gets a bit corrupted in our human experience.

We have an unhealthy bond with our parents when we cannot make a decision without wondering if they would approve. This is different than seeking their wise input.

We have an unhealthy bond with our children when their behaviour dictates our self-worth or sense of well-being. This is much different than wanting them to make good choices for their own good.

We have an unhealthy bond with our spouse when their inability to meet our needs leaves us feeling devastated, out of kilter, or angry.

Life is going to be better when our relationships function according to God's design, but our children, parents, and spouses cannot bear the weight of living under the expectation of doing that perfectly. When we break unhealthy ties in these relationships, we aren't cutting off or abandoning the other person. We bless them and keep the good and healthy bonds.

Any time I find myself persistently wondering what so-and-so would think about a decision or something I've done or said, it's a clue for me that I'm developing an unhealthy tie with them. Though wise input and feedback are incredibly helpful, it's unhealthy to give too much weight to one person's opinion.

When I have a disproportionate reaction to my husband's approval or lack thereof, I know that I have moved into unhealthy attachment. When one of my children has a bad day and slams their door, making me feel rejected, I know that I'm giving away my "okay-ness." Why? Because as valuable as each of these people may be in my life, they cannot take the place of God.

What does God have to say about my thoughts and actions? Humans are helpful, but not perfect. God says that we need each other, but how do we do this well? It's hard to stay connected without expecting too much. It's hard to remain lovingly present when our needs aren't being met.

As you've been reading, I hope you're experiencing some curiosity about your relationships. Do you have unwanted reoccurring dreams about anyone? Has someone passed away, leaving you to feel like you're still haemorrhaging pain? Do you find yourself constantly seeking a certain individual's approval? Are you jerked around by the opinions of others? Ask Jesus if there's anyone with whom you have an unhealthy bond.

My friend Dean heard this teaching and had the thought that by definition he probably had an unhealthy bond with his mom even though that didn't seem logically true to his brain. He went ahead and went through the steps of breaking this unhealthy tie and the impact on his marriage was immediately obvious to both him and his wife.

Jesus knows stuff we don't. He's the great Architect of our restoration. What is He saying to you right now?

THE TOOL

This tool has a unique variation, depending on the nature of the relationship to which it is applied. If you apply it to an ongoing relationship that you want to lean in to, you will specify that you're breaking unhealthy ties and bless the ongoing relationship. If you're applying it to a relationship that's over, you will break *all* ties. If the relationship was sexual or physical in any way, you will want to include bodily ties as well as soul ties.

I always begin by placing the cross of Jesus between me and the person with whom I have the tie. It's a great visual. The cross of Jesus is the point of redemption. It's the place where anything broken or dissonant is recalibrated, the place where we bring our own brokenness and the debt of others. The work of the cross holds our relationships together, as they're a work in progress.

If you are uncomfortable with this visual for now, that's okay. Simply move on to the next part.

Invoking the name of Jesus in this step is to acknowledge His presence and power. He is the only one who has the power to save us from our past and restore the damage that has been done by others.

Before you can break these unhealthy ties, you must first forgive the other party or receive grace for yourself. Definitely take the time to go back to that step if needed before proceeding.

For a relationship that is *over*, pray the following out loud:

I place the cross of Jesus Christ between me and _____.

In the name of Jesus, I break all ties formed between us. (If the relationship was physical, break all "spirit, soul, and body ties.")

In the name of Jesus, I send back to _____ all parts of themself that they gave to me. In the name of Jesus, I take back from _____ all parts of myself that I gave to them.

Holy Spirit of God, please set a watch over my soul to keep me from forming any unhealthy ties with them again.

For a relationship that is *ongoing*, pray the following out loud:

I place the cross of Jesus Christ between me and _____.
In the name of Jesus, I break any and all unhealthy ties formed between us.

In the name of Jesus, I send back to _____ all parts of themself that they gave to me outside of God's design.

In the name of Jesus, I take back from _____ all parts of myself that I gave to them outside God's design.

I bless and I keep the relationship God has for us.

Holy Spirit of God, please set a watch over my soul to keep me from forming any unhealthy ties with them again.

Breathe deeply. Release the other person. Receive wholeness for yourself. Ask Jesus if there's anything He wants you to know about this relationship.

HERE'S HOPE

The courageous step of releasing another person from the obligation to meet your needs makes space for Jesus to fill. He is surer and more solid than anyone you have ever met.

Don't be overwhelmed if you feel like you have a long list of unhealthy bonds. Jesus is gentle. As you take the time to work through each one, you will regain parts of yourself that you didn't even know were missing.

Your resilience will increase. Energy and joy will rise. You were made for love, freely given and freely received.

AMY'S
STORY

THE MOST EXTRAORDINARY STORY I KNOW REGARDING UNHEALTHY
soul ties belongs to my good friend Amy. I find this delightful, since she
is one of the most rational and analytical people I know. It's beautiful because the effect was so powerful. Something very broken was restored.
Here it is in Amy's own words.

I had heard of soul ties before, but I had relegated them into the
sphere of "those Christians." You know, the ones on the weird
end of the spectrum. Certainly, objective and rational people
like me didn't put much stock in soul ties.

That was my position until breaking an ungodly soul tie
healed my body.

For as long as I can remember, I had abnormal menstrual cycles. Whether in level of pain, length, flow, etc., it was
never healthy.

After the birth of my two children, it got worse. While
the pain level wasn't off the charts, the length and flow certainly were. I was on a two-weeks-on/two-weeks-off cycle and my
flow wasn't healthy. This was impacting my life in every way—
physically, emotionally, relationally, and sexually.

I pursued various medical inquiries and interventions, but
no definitive cause was ever found. In fact, my doctor told me
that some people just have weird periods and I would just have
to live with it.

I had an endometrial ablation, which did nothing to solve
the issues. So I finally resigned myself to just live with it.

During this time, I leaned into what Jesus had for me and began learning how to have a healthy soul.

I ended up at a prayer ministry course. One of the sessions was on soul ties. I sat through the whole session feeling very sceptical and unsure.

For the activation piece, the instructors had us ask Jesus who we needed to break soul ties with. I got three names, two of which don't pertain to this story. The third one was a girl with whom I had shared sexual exploration when I was in Kindergarten. At this point, the event wasn't a secret and I had already done all the things I knew to be important—confession, repentance, forgiveness, etc.

I am, for the most part, a rule follower. So even though I was unsure about this whole soul tie thing, breaking unhealthy soul ties was part of the course curriculum and I was going to complete the course guidelines.

I went through the process of breaking unhealthy soul ties with this girl and right away a thought popped into my head: "Your bleeding issues are done." I wasn't even thinking about that anymore. I had tucked that away into the never-going-to-change box.

But here's the thing about the name of Jesus and the power of the cross: never-going-to-change doesn't exist there.

My bleeding issues were done! A regular menstrual cycle was restored the very next month and has continued throughout all the years since then.

HERITAGE ROCKS

Chapter Seventeen

There is no transformation without confession. There is no victory in hiding. There is no breakthrough in secrecy.[20]

—Rob Reimer

I HAVE A FRIEND WHO'S A GRAIN FARMER. DAN GROWS WHEAT, BARLEY, canola, and fescue on land that he inherited from his father. Any time he tills his fields, rocks come to the surface. He jokes that his land grows more rocks than anything else. His family isn't amused, though, as this means they get to do their least favourite chore: rock-picking. Rock-picking is tedious, back-aching work that seems endless.

Where did these rocks come from? They're ancient. They were there long before my farmer friend came on the scene. Yet they are now his problem.

And there's no point in him being annoyed at his father for not removing them all. His father did what he could in his time. Yet they keep surfacing and another generation must deal with them.

Our souls are a little bit like these fields. We've inherited some wonderful things and also some things that are definitely not wonderful. Like Dan, we can cultivate the goodness in our inheritance, but we must also deal with the rocks left by previous generations. We could leave them for another generation to deal with, but they will bust up machinery and limit our fruitfulness.

Generational blessings and curses are part of everyone's story. No family is too messed up to be devoid of blessings—though you may have to look pretty hard in some—nor is any family so splendid that you cannot find a theme of the strategy against fruitfulness.

God loves family. It was His idea in the first place. Anything He has made is beautiful and good, and therefore worthy of the assault of the enemy who is jealous of anything powerful or glorious.

Each one of us has shown up in a family line of one generation after another that has made choices leading up to the moment in which we find ourselves. Our ancestors have made decisions about whether they're going to take the bait laid out by the enemy and respond to brokenness with more brokenness. Or maybe they'll surrender to the love and leadership of their Holy Advocate in response to the inevitable pain that comes from being born into a world at war.

However, we aren't simply victims or lottery winners. The baton has been passed to us and the race we run is going to leave a legacy. This is empowering and exciting!

As an individual reading this book right now, you are made up of physical, mental, emotional, and spiritual parts that are all interconnected. Furthermore, all those aspects of your being have been shaped and influenced by your family story, which is generations long. You really are an amazing, one-of-a-kind being with unique traits, personality, and talents. No one else can be you. Your restored expression of the Creator is quite dangerous to the strategies of the enemy—therefore, it is under assault.

I think it's necessary to take the time to consider our heritage for the simple reason that the gifts and talents that run in our family are a blessing to be cultivated, and that the strategies of the enemy against us are so familiar that it can be hard to recognize them and easy to succumb. In fact, they're so normal to us that it's often a surprise to discover that we can live without them.

Any time I address this, there are two challenges. Some cultures worship and venerate their ancestors, which makes it hard to acknowledge and deal with the broken parts of their family story. Other cultures are quick to blame and shame their parents for every challenge they've ever faced.

Neither posture is helpful, and frankly each is destructive in its own way. The most honouring thing we can do for our family is acknowledge and overcome destructive patterns and celebrate and cultivate the gifts of our heritage.

If you feel defensive right now, I would encourage you to simply take a deep breath. This isn't about throwing anyone under the bus. This isn't about shame—not on you or your family. This is about courageously shifting the trajectory of your family line.

Consider your physical self right now. Who do you see? My hands remind me of both my mother and my Oma. The shape of my nails is so much like my mother's nails. Every time I look at my fingers, I see my paternal grandmother's hands. The crinkles around my eyes remind me of my paternal aunt's laughter. The shape of my eyebrows is just like my mom's and her sister's. Two family lines have converged in me, a single unique person.

Now consider the makeup of your disposition. This gets a little more nuanced. One side of my family lived through two World Wars. This led to feelings of anxiety and a sense of scarcity. This side of my family also has a tremendous sense of humour and an ability to find joy in the silly details of life. They are incredibly hard-working and I love the work ethic they've passed on to me.

This is a generational blessing that can be twisted through generational anxiety. How much hard work is enough? Does my hard work feed pride and self-reliance or is it fruitful and glorifying to my Creator? Is my sense of humour a source of joy or a lighthearted but sneaky agent of cynicism? The enemy of our souls is always trying to mess with a good thing.

On the other side of my family, the strategies of the enemy are a little more obvious. Mental illness is hard to hide, even more so when it leads to murder. Then it all becomes wrapped up in a tarp of shame—and shame breeds fear faster than fruit flies multiply. What if, what if, what if! What if people find out… what if I don't have what it takes… what if I'm going to turn out like this, too?

I had such mixed feelings about being with this side of my family when I was a child. Poverty and sadness are tangible. Grimy. They smell like nicotine and cooking grease.

The weight of it was so familiar that it was impossible to deny deep inside me. This is who I was, too, even if I could show up elsewhere all shiny.

But this side of my family is also incredibly kind and compassionate. They are very creative—musicians, artists, stained-glass workers, woodcarvers—and I think this generational blessing shows up in my love of beautifully crafted words. They have no problem venturing off the beaten track, and I have discovered amazing things off the beaten track. I have poignant memories of corn boils on the beach and guitars strumming in the darkness. Sadness and sweetness all mixed together. Complicated.

All of this produced me, a muddle of hard work and heavy-hearted lethargy. Humour and tears. Beauty and pain. Highs and lows. Sometimes it has felt like a tug of war in the core of my being. Actually, there is one!

In order for me to flourish in hope, I needed to clearly identify the heritage rocks in my soul and deal with them. I didn't know I could fling them out of the field of my heart. With these rocks out the way, my soul would break into the sparkling beauty of spring. Ancient seeds would have room to bust open and bear fruit.

Most of us know that junk runs in our family and we try to deal with it, but if we do it in the wrong way it seems as though it just brings up more rocks, and farming around all these obstacles takes a lot of energy. The child of an alcoholic vows they'll never be an alcoholic, but instead they become a workaholic. Same rock, just hammered into a different shape.

The problem with trying to address these rocks with our own grit and determination is that we try to become god in our own lives. It's better than nothing, but there is a better way.

ROCK WALLS

Stan was the youngest of several children. About the time his older siblings were moving out, one of his parents had an affair and left home, too. This was incredibly painful and left him feeling abandoned and alone.

He was understandably angry. He made a lot of judgments and vowed that he would never do anything like that.

Several years later, another family member had an affair and Stan became even more irate. How could they have done that knowing how much pain infidelity causes?!

You can probably imagine what happened next.

A year later, Stan was really struggling with depression. He was out of work when a former co-worker sent him a flirtatious text. He responded in kind. One thing led to another until the messages were clearly sexual in nature.

When Stan's wife found out, he refused to acknowledge that this was infidelity. After all, he wasn't like his family. Or at least not as bad. His refusal to face his own weakness and take responsibility caused a lot of damage to his marriage.

You see, pushing a rock of judgment up against the rock of infidelity didn't remove it. By making a vow that he'd never be like other members of his family, he just stacked another rock on top. Yet another rock in the pile was one of self-righteousness, which through my years of working with people I've found to be sinful and unhelpful.

Before you know it, you can build a wall of rocks in the middle of your field, a barrier rather than fertile open space. You can consume a lot of energy piling up rocks of protection rather than cultivating freedom. We don't make ourselves safe with vows, judgments, and accusations. So what on earth do we do?

The way of restoration is often counterintuitive. In Stan's story, the first step was to make a healthy lament. The rest of the tools are the same we've already explored. When it comes to generational pain, acknowledge that you've inherited it. Are there specific individuals who have perpetuated this pain? You need to forgive them. Name the action and the pain. Identify the judgments and vows you've made. These must be revoked. Bring them to Jesus and repent of making them. Speak blessing over your family line.

Next, ask Jesus, your restoration Architect, to show you how this pain shows up in your life. Remember, the enemy of your soul is often very sneaky because you're too smart to be tricked by something obvious.

Shame and pride keep us from wanting to acknowledge this pain, but the pathway to flourishing comes through humility. The safest way forward is to humbly acknowledge that we, too, are capable of the same things as other members of our family. Perhaps we are even likely to continue down the same generational paths.

Pride resists the work of God in our lives whereas humility invites grace. When we're willing to name our own susceptibility, we put it firmly in the crosshairs and can deal with it.

In Stan's story, seduction offered comfort and excitement when life was hard. We're particularly vulnerable to falling into old family ruts when we go through seasons of difficulty. If he had acknowledged this and addressed it at the first whiff, he would have been spared a lot of pain. He didn't need to embrace his propensity to cheat, but he did need to acknowledge the weakness. Secrecy was not his friend. Confession and humility would have set him free and made his marriage strong. Shame says, "I'm a terrible person because I struggle with this." Humility says, "I need help with this." Break agreement with family shame. Choose humility.

In my story, it seemed that I was being strangled by twin strands of fear and hopelessness. Both were so logical and had so much evidence to support them that it simply didn't seem there was another way to live. The posture of victimhood came naturally. I would honestly have said I was born that way, so did that make these twin tormentors an inevitable way of life for me?

I knew there had been abuse and neglect in my family that had caused tremendous pain. I believe this is the root of much of the mental illness in our family. Even though I have a really wonderful father who was protective and empowering, my soul still seemed marked by the fallout of generations of brokenness.

There is an age-old question that asks whether we are shaped by nature or nurture. Neuroscience and epigenetics reveal fascinating truth about this. Had I inherited genetic material that was altered by abuse? Perhaps. Had I been shaped by attitudes that were formed by the thinking of generations of abusers and abused? Probably.

Yet I had the capacity to make choices that could alter the trajectory of my life. I could begin to think about what I was thinking about, thereby bringing my thoughts into alignment with the new reality of my healing journey. I forgave those I know of and those I didn't for abusing the women they had been assigned to protect. I forgave them for not cherishing us and fighting for us. I broke agreement with so many things... the lie that I'd been abandoned, that I had to fight for myself, that there was no hope, that fear offered protection, that men could rarely be trusted, and that it sucked to be a woman.

There were so many layers and nuances for me to deal with. I came to recognize that it was easy for me to fall back on these patterns of thought, so I needed to be diligent in cultivating the seeds of truth Jesus gave to me in their place.

Something began to bloom in my soul. Hope. Courage. My posture changed.

Something else really interesting happened. For as long as I could remember, men had randomly hit on me. I once wondered if I had an invisible sign on my back that said, "Grab me." Of course I wondered if this was somehow my fault.

Some time after I forgave my ancestors and broke agreement with the lie that I was a victim and men were all out to use me, I realized that this had stopped happening. It never has happened again. Not one more time. Something happened in an unseen dimension to have a radical impact on my tangible experience.

I still have to be vigilant about hopelessness and anxiety. It can sneak up on me in dozens of ways, and I hardly notice this happening because it's so familiar and logical to me. But it's no longer the stronghold it once was. Now it's a pothole—and when I recognize it, I can move on quite easily. It's easy to fall back into generational patterns, but when we've trained our souls in a new way it's also a short trip back.

The great risk when dealing with our generational challenges is in either overestimating or underestimating the impact it has in our lives. In thinking we're above the temptations of our ancestors, we can overlook the insidious ways in which patterns sneak in. The other ditch we can fall into is thinking that this is inevitable, that these patterns will always be the same in our family story. How do we stay on the road that leads forward?

THE TOOL

All the tools we've covered so far come together here.

Consider your family story and allow yourself to be curious about how the common themes have shown up in your life. As Jesus shows you things you might rather not think about, choose humility.

The pathway forward comes through healthy grieving about what has happened to you as well as the ways in which you have participated in your family's brokenness. We've all done it.

Forgive family members for perpetuating patterns of brokenness and for leaving those rocks for you to clear.

Break agreement with the lies you have believed and the judgments you have made. Surrender the vows made in your own strength. Ask Jesus what He has for you to plant in the place of these ancient rocks.

Be honest with those closest to you about the potholes left in your life because of generational patterns. Feel no shame, only courage.

HERE'S HOPE

It's not too late for you or your family to start walking a new path. It may have taken generations to arrive at the place you currently find yourself, but a small step in a new direction today will take you to a radically different place down the road. It will affect the generations to come.

The generational blessings in your family are probably a greater force than you realize. The small steps you're taking as you progress through this book are going to catapult you forward. You were designed to flourish creatively. As you remove blockages and barriers, thriving is inevitable.

NOT
GOOD?

Chapter Eighteen

It's not good for the Man to be alone; I'll make him a helper, a companion.

—Genesis 2:18, MSG

SO FAR YOU'VE READ CHAPTER AFTER CHAPTER ABOUT DEALING WITH the fallout of broken relationships. One could start to wonder if our safest bet is to simply hide out, hunker down, or run away.

The Genesis account of creation tells of God and the first man, Adam, being in a perfect space together. Adam didn't have to drag himself out of bed every morning and go to work. He didn't wonder what kind of mood his boss might be in or if he was ever going to get a raise. He didn't even have to get dressed! He could simply stroll through the garden and pick a fresh papaya or a handful of grapes. If it was truly paradise, he was probably figuring out how to brew the perfect cup of coffee from the world's most pristine beans. I picture him scratching a lion behind the ears while he waited for the drip. Chatting up the Trinity. Basking in the sun. Birds singing. No fear. No scarcity. No strife. No wedgies and no worries. Perfect peace and contentment.

Almost perfect. It seems that when Adam noticed the animals pairing up, he found himself with a restless longing for something or someone.

Then God dropped a bomb that changed everything. In this perfect space, God declared there was something "not good"—that it was not good for Adam to be alone.

Any time something isn't good, God has a plan, because He's all about goodness. So God told Adam that He was going to make a companion who was *"just right"* for him (Genesis 2:2).

Now, I'm going to be very honest with you. The most profound pain I've experienced has come from human interactions. Many days, I thought the best possible version of life would be just me and Jesus hanging out back in paradise. Yet God said that is "not good," so something must be wildly out of whack in my current circumstances.

It is. In me. And in the people around me.

We are not in Kansas anymore. Or paradise. Adam and Eve screwed up, and when they were caught they threw each other under the bus. Humans have been trapped in this cycle ever since. Unless they jump off the hamster wheel and surrender to the hard work of restoration, this cycle is inevitable.

Some of the sweetest moments of intimacy I've ever experienced have happened within the context of marriage. Our marriage has also been the backdrop for some of my greatest pain. The sweet moments have taken place when we tasted what God originally designed for us. The worst moments have taken place when our broken places collided.

We didn't anticipate these moments on our sparkling thirty-below-zero, six-feet-of-snow January wedding day. We knew there would be challenges, of course, but we were sure we had what it would take to get through.

We weren't wrong, but we had no idea how hard it would be. We'd be going along fine and all of a sudden seemingly step on a landmine. Anger like an explosion. Words like shrapnel. Carnage in our souls. We'd stagger around dazed and confused for a few days until we "got over" it and then we'd be fine again.

Until the next time.

The cycle soon became obvious. I lived in so much anxiety about setting off another landmine.

God may have said it's "not good" for us to be alone, but being together sure wasn't good either. How could two smart, kind, intelligent, wise, funny, hard-working people end up in this situation?

I begged for marriage counselling to no avail. I cried out to God to heal our marriage or get me out of it somehow. We had three beautiful kids and so much worth fighting for, but it felt like the best I could do was hope to avoid accidentally triggering a crisis. This terrible state of anxiety wasn't good for my physical or emotional health. Every single reader knows this is dysfunctional. I had lost hope of any other solution. I had three healthy miracle babies, a nice home, and a hard-working but emotionally distant husband. I wasn't okay. I was desperate. If God didn't do something, I was going to fall apart in a million pieces… and I knew that would perpetuate a cycle of brokenness.

God never ignores our pleas; it's just that His answers aren't always packaged the way we hope. He was gently leading me down a pathway of healing. I wanted Him to "beam me up," and he wanted to wrap me up in His love and teach me how to live in a new way.

I started to recognize a theme in these relational landmines. When the pain in my soul bumped into the pain in his soul, we had nothing to offer each other except more pain.

His story involves a distant and eventually absent father, which led him to make vows that he didn't need anyone. This triggered the great pain of abandonment in my soul. He couldn't see it; clearly, it was my problem. I could see he had a problem, and I thought if he fixed it our problems would be solved. I did a terrible job of trying to communicate this. In reality, we both had a problem, broken places that needed an encounter with the Healer. We were both trying really hard, but we needed more than what our good intentions could produce.

I felt so helpless and hopeless. The gift in this mess is that it propelled me forward in the very painful and hard work of restoration. I couldn't make him work on his stuff—that wasn't my job—but I could work on mine. Slowly I began to see that as I reached for Jesus, when the agony of abandonment threatened to overwhelm me, the landmines came less often. I still felt pain, and things were still broken, but I no longer reacted to that pain with accusation. I ran to Jesus and gave Him my pain.

Please don't imagine a lovely Hollywood scene of just the right lighting and music. It was messy. Our very real pain is gritty. It was a case of shedding blood, sweat, and tears. Jesus literally met me every single time and wrapped me in love.

I would use the tools I've described in these pages. I would forgive my husband for the things he had knowingly or unknowingly done to cause me pain. I would break agreement with every lie that had felt so true. I would breathe in the truth Jesus was giving me—put my feet into it, wiggle roots down deep, and grow stronger and more resilient. I would still feel pain, but I'd no longer be undone by it.

Something mysterious and sweet began to happen. Remember the courtroom scene in Chapter Thirteen? Each time I went through this grieving-forgiving-breaking-agreement-soul-tie-releasing process, I removed myself from the position of the accuser. I would look to Jesus and trust that He was going to pay the debt that I perceived was owed to me. I would release my husband Brian to Jesus, release him of obligations, release him of the judgments I was making.

Rather than expecting him to meet needs he actually couldn't meet, I began to encounter Jesus in that space. This didn't mean there were no boundaries, that he didn't have responsibilities as my husband, or that there was no need for communication. It meant I could show up in those conversations with a very different posture and tone.

Not surprisingly, this completely changed the dynamics of our interactions. You can imagine how Brian gained more space to breathe without being on the receiving end of my pain-filled expectations and accusations. Somehow it became easier for him to see areas where he needed to grow and change, too.

The enemy of our souls had been preying on our wounds and we'd become locked in a dance that looked more like a wrestling match. As each of us stopped seeing the other as the enemy and recognized the work of the real enemy, we made space for God's Spirit to move in our relationship.

I've focused on our marriage in this chapter because it has been the crucible of my learning, but these principles apply to all relationships. Broken places collide in our families, workspaces, schools, teams, and communities. The answer isn't to run away or shut down. God said that it isn't good to be alone. We need each other, but we won't thrive in relationship without growing in spiritual and emotional health.

One person cannot singlehandedly heal a marriage or any other relationship, but they can make a big difference. God doesn't leave us at the mercy of the choices of another person. He makes a way for our healing. Our growth actually makes space for the healing the other person needs. We don't heal each other. We don't complete each other. Every encounter we have with Jesus fills us with more of His love and our healing becomes contagious. We become agents of restoration in our sphere of influence.

Whether your struggle is with your spouse, in-laws, siblings, or co-workers, you can find clues to restoration in recognizing where your broken places collide. You can bring your broken places to the Healer. He will give you compassion for all that brokenness. Then use the tools laid out in the previous chapters. He will give you strategies for moving forward.

God is the one who said it isn't good to be alone—and when something isn't good, He has a plan.

THE TOOL

If you recognize the dynamic of broken places colliding, take the time to process a lament of your pain and frustrations. Forgive and break agreement with lies. Break unhealthy soul ties. Get honest about your own broken places and invite Jesus to do His work of restoration.

HERE'S HOPE

Like Eve, you were created "just right" for relationship. The beauty of that original design is breathtaking. Actually, it's dangerous. In sync, we fight for each other rather than with each other. We have each other's back. Our differences lend strength to the other and enrich our shared experiences.

The enemy of our souls hates this so much because his one plan is destruction.

I bless you with all the courage you need to allow Jesus to restore your soul back to its original glory. He is gentle and knows exactly what you need in order to learn how to dance in a new way. It will be awkward at first, but it will become smoother and more graceful with practice.

WHERE'S JESUS?

Chapter Nineteen

I will never leave you or abandon you.

—Jesus

DEAR READER, YOU HAVE COME SO FAR IN DOING THE MESSY, awkward, painful, holy work of daring to peel back the bandages and callouses on your soul. You've braved the stench, the pus, and the pain. You've fiercely pushed through and removed the junk, cleansed the infection, and removed the fetters.

Now what? What of that wound? Do we live the rest of our lives carefully guarding it? Is there any way to move forward with our heads up, walking with a free and easy stride? Must you simply move ahead doing the best you can in spite of your past?

There is even more goodness ahead of you. There is healing—really. Your story will always shape you, but you can be defined by what Jesus did for you rather than whatever else has happened in your life. The highlights can be your healing rather than your trauma.

You thought the climax of your story was the day you failed epically, the day they walked out on you, the day you got the diagnosis, the day of the great sadness, or simply a long tunnel of grey, but there's something ahead of you that's better than you thought possible.

If you've engaged with the process I have been laying out, you've been sorting through the impact and effect of both the seen and unseen players on the stage of your story. You've unravelled lies, released others through forgiveness, received grace for your screwups, cast off unhealthy bonds, and invited the Architect of your restoration to arrange things in a new way.

Picture yourself at centre stage of your story. Nothing else on the stage is in the same place it was several chapters ago. Now what?

It's time for a hero to step into the scene. Perhaps you've been thinking that you are the hero of your story—and it's true that you have bravely pushed forward—but in the best stories the main character could never have triumphed without that other person in their life. David had Jonathan. Batman had Robin. Frodo had Sam. Tom Sawyer had Huck Finn. Sherlock Holmes had Dr. Watson. Luke Skywalker had Obi-Wan Kenobi. Calvin had Hobbes!

As much as any of us might prefer to go it alone, there is also a desire to be part of one of these dynamic duos. We long to know that someone has our back, that someone would stick with us even when they know our weakness. We ache to be loved so much that another person would actually take a bullet for us.

Jesus wants to be that One for you, and so much more. He wants to rewrite your past, infuse your present, and meet you in your future.

Before you dismiss this as a cheesy Sunday school pleasantry, please pause and ponder the possibility of that literally becoming true for you. Jesus is *"the exact expression of God's true nature—his mirror image"* (Hebrews 1:3, TPT). No other human in your life has fully demonstrated His perfect love for you, although if you're lucky you've had a few who have given you a glimpse.

If you live on the earth, God has also been misrepresented to you in some way. If you want to know what God is like, you need to know Jesus. The way to know Him best is to read the Gospels. Picture yourself in those stories.

Jesus is so wonderful that it's impossible to describe Him with just one metaphor. He is described as a lover pursuing his beloved. A friend who is closer than a brother. A big brother paving the way for younger siblings. A champion who fights for the oppressed.

Who do you need Him to be in your story? Other than your fairy godmother, of course! He wants to meet you in your place of need and lead you to a place of victory. It's not that you can just make Him conform to your image of who you want Him to be, but that He now waits for an invitation from you to come centre stage.

Because I have struggled with a sense of being emotionally abandoned, I have longed to know Him as the relentless lover of my soul. I have needed to know Him as ever-present and interested. In trauma and tragedy, I have needed to know Him as a protector who will hold me and fight for me. When I have messed up, I have needed to know Him as one who will take a bullet for me. He is all of these things, but He doesn't barge in. He waits to be invited.

Healing happens when we recognize that He has been all we need and more on every page of our story. He has always been there. He's not turned away or indifferent. He's not angry or annoyed. Many of us have been trained to assent to this truth theologically, on an intellectual level. But healing happens when we *experience* it as true.

The facts of our stories—the things we can touch, taste, see, feel, and smell—have defined our experiences. The enemy of our souls has ridden on all those facts and delivered lies about who we are and who God is. All the hard work you have done so far has cleared away much of the rubble that would block your awareness of Jesus. The next step is to invite Him to show you His presence in the defining moments of your life.

The first time I did this, I admit I was really sceptical, even a little embarrassed, but I had signed up for this healing retreat and no one would ever need to know I had tried something so weird. Feeling ridiculous, I asked Jesus to show me where He had been all those times when I'd felt so alone.

Immediately I pictured my childhood kitchen. I was sitting with crayons and paper at a yellow child-sized table and chairs I had forgotten we ever had. Very alone. And then I saw Jesus sitting on the other chair, looking at me with total adoration. He smiled at my colouring like it was the most wonderful masterpiece.

Suddenly I sobbed. Big, heaving gasps of sadness were being washed away in tenderness.

I couldn't have made this up, neither the picture nor the response. It wasn't mere emotionalism. Something stored deep inside me was experiencing a radical shift in reality. All my other experiences had shaped my understanding of my place in the world, but there had been something missing. I had not been alone. Someone else was there. Someone who adored me.

That small moment changed everything, and not for just a moment. Nothing has been quite the same since.

This must beg a question or two. Was I simply making this up? Was it just mental gymnastics creating a feel-good moment?

First of all, this memory wasn't one I chose to retrieve, though the exercise will work for those memories also. Second, it's consistent with the nature and character of Jesus. We have firsthand accounts of His delight in children. In fact, He gave a stern scolding to some of His friends who treated children like an inconvenience (Mark 10:13–16). Scripture is chockfull of affirmations that He takes delight in His children, that He'll never abandon them, that He is always with them.

Second, research shows that memories aren't consolidated in long-term storage. When memories are retrieved, they become unstable and malleable. In these moments a memory can be "disrupted or updated and transformed… each time a memory is recalled it can be weakened, strengthened, or otherwise modified during reconsolidation."[21] When I retrieved this memory and updated it with significant missing information, I didn't distort the memory. Rather, it was clarified.

The trick to this step, if there is one, is that you must know the true nature and character of God because the enemy of your soul is always present and trying to bring distortion.

Chloe was attending a workshop where this was being taught. When she asked Jesus to speak to her, she sensed nothing but scolding and accusation. It was intense and she became very distressed.

This nattering was definitely the voice of her enemy. I knew it couldn't be Jesus, because when we read firsthand accounts of His behaviour He was always moved with compassion when people came to Him humbly. He was fierce with people who were proud and oppressing others but tender with those who came to Him aware of their need, *always* healing and restoring them.

Chloe's marriage was a disaster and she had come to the workshop longing for it to be healed. We found a quiet place together and asked the Holy Spirit, the engineer of her restoration, why she thought God was angry with her. She knew immediately, but it was a secret she had kept buried for decades.

Dark secrets always give the enemy access to our souls. We cannot experience freedom and healing until we bring them into the light.

Chloe spent several moments wrestling with the risk of bringing this event to light. Thankfully her desperation trumped shame and she shared with us that she and her brother had engaged in some sexual behaviour together in their early teens. She had mentally tucked it away as a stupid thing kids do, but it was a stronghold of shame and unhealthy bonds. We worked through forgiving her brother, receiving grace for herself, breaking agreement with shame and perversion, and severing the unhealthy bonds that had formed through the sexual encounter and shared secret. Then she asked Jesus again, "What do You want me to know?"

I wish everyone could experience these moments. All doubt that this is somehow manufactured doesn't stand a chance in the beauty of what happens when the truth of God's huge, extravagant love comes flooding in. Chloe was undone as laughter and tears mingled in a healing flow. She was loved! This secret had lost all its power. She knew that she was loved and that Jesus had been there with His arms open, aching for their loss, making a way for restoration, and just waiting for her to receive all that He had for her.

Chloe became a force. She declared freedom everywhere she went. Her marriage was restored. Nothing was the same after she experienced this healing encounter with Jesus.

Would you like to invite Jesus into some of your memories? When we surrender our agenda of having Him show up like a fairy godmother, when we clear away bitterness and lies and invite Him into our story, we are better able to experience His presence.

Take one of the scenarios you've already processed while journeying through this book. As the memory surfaces, ask Jesus to show you where He was, what He wants to say to you, and what He would like you to know. He will show up in a way that's meaningful to you.

If you're struggling to experience Him in this moment, ask Him if anything is blocking your experience of His presence. You may need to go back to some of the earlier steps and process something.

It may be that this is simply such a new experience for you that you need to prime the pump a bit. You can do this by reading an account of Jesus interacting with someone and imagining yourself in the story. Then take it a step further and imagine Him in your story. Based on the first-hand accounts in the New Testament, how is Jesus likely to approach you? What is He likely to say?

THE TOOL

In the sixteenth century, a priest and theologian named Ignatius Loyola developed the spiritual practice of Gospel contemplation in order to help people experience the reality of Jesus within their own stories.

You can try it now with the following steps. Then you can take it a step further and invite Jesus to show you His presence in your own story.

Step one. Keeping in mind that the Holy Spirit is present with you, read the following account twice so the story and details become familiar.

> *Late that night, the disciples were in their boat in the middle of the lake, and Jesus was alone on land. He saw that they were in serious trouble, rowing hard and struggling against the wind and waves. About three o'clock in the morning Jesus came toward them, walking on the water. He intended to go past them, but when they saw him walking on the water, they cried out in terror, thinking he was a ghost. They were all terrified when they saw him.*
>
> *But Jesus spoke to them at once. "Don't be afraid," he said. "Take courage! I am here!" Then he climbed into the boat, and the wind stopped. They were totally amazed...*
>
> —Mark 6:47–51

Step two. Close your eyes and imagine the story. Picture the storm. Feel the wind and waves. What are people saying? Where is Jesus? Imagine seeing Him and feeling afraid, but then He calls out with words of comfort. Do not be afraid.

Step three. Think about a "storm" you're currently experiencing in your life. What details feel like wind and waves? How do you feel as you are being tossed about in the middle of this storm? Picture Jesus coming toward you with His hand out. Hear Him say, "Do not be afraid. Take courage. I am here." Whisper these words. Invite Him into the boat with you. Breathe deeply as the waves calm. Ask Him what He wants you to know about this storm.

I bless you to experience His presence in this moment.

Now go back to one of the experiences you've already processed and ask Jesus to show you where He was in that moment. Relax and receive from Him.

HERE'S HOPE

Jesus has always been with you and He wants you to know His presence. The enemy of your soul will do everything he can to keep you from knowing God's love, but he is not more powerful than Jesus.

NO MORE
TORMENT

Chapter Twenty

The God of peace will soon crush Satan under your feet.

—Romans 16:20

I WOULD MAKE A TERRIBLE WITNESS IN ANY POLICE INVESTIGATION.
The interview would go something like this.

"Ma'am, can you describe the assailant?"

"Um, he was kinda tall and maybe had brownish hair. I'm pretty sure
he's really sad. He feels like people think he's stupid and he gets angry and
wants to prove that he's really smart."

Raised eyebrows and quizzical looks. Try picking that out of a lineup.

All my life I've had sort of a radar for what people are feeling. Whenever I walk into a space, I sense things in the atmosphere. When I was
quite young, I just started experiencing the feelings of others.

As I grew a little older and recognized that I easily acted out what
I sensed in others, I got hard on myself for "being so easily led." I felt like
there was something terribly wrong with me.

It was also exhausting. Dealing with my own feelings was more than
enough work without also feeling what everyone else in the room was
going through. Sometimes I would "see" things, too—ugly, contorted crea-
tures that seemed to be there but weren't. Or were they? Maybe I was
crazy. After all, crazy runs in the family.

I didn't realize that this was a gift, and I didn't know what I could do
with it. It felt like a curse.

However, when the Creator picked blue eyes and dimples for me, He
also saw fit to bestow a gift of discernment. It wasn't always a bad thing.

Sometimes I also saw beautiful beings and felt waves of love and beauty. It's just that I felt jerked around by whatever was going on around me.

When I was a kid, people didn't talk much about the supernatural, but it's mainstream now. Many top-rated television series focus on the supernatural. Most teens I talk to are quite comfortable admitting that they see otherworldly beings, especially at night. They seem quick to accept the fact that there's a spirit world, but sometimes they're reluctant to engage with taking authority over their spiritual atmosphere.

As I learned the things I share in this book, I gained a lot of clarity about those unseen characters on the stage of my story. I began to unravel what was me and what was being sent to me from other sources.

I met other people with a similar gift and we learned from each other. I embraced it as a gift because I came to understand that everything dark must bow to the authority of Jesus in me. Jesus defeated darkness. He hates torment. He wants His beautiful creation to be free, released from torment and unleashed to flourish. This seeing and feeling could clarify what was tormenting people and help set them free. It's a gift that is only helpful if it's motivated by love, but He provides that, too.

Early one Saturday morning, I got a call from a dear friend. She and her husband had experienced a terrible night and her husband felt like he was going crazy. She was terribly sorry to bother me but wondered if I could meet with them because they were at their wits' end.

I agreed to meet with them at my office right away. I knew they weren't the type to call on a Saturday morning unless they were truly desperate.

Her husband Reg is one of the nicest guys I know. He's a rough and tumble oilpatch worker with a heart of gold. He likes to make a show of having no tender feelings, but he'd give you the coat off his back in half a minute.

When Reg walked into my office, my heart broke for him. I understood exactly what was going on. He told me that, for as long as he could remember, he'd been having flashes of violent images flit through his mind, including murderous thoughts. It was terrible. He'd never told anyone because he was afraid it would get him locked up, but the situation had gotten so bad recently that he was truly afraid he was losing his mind. He didn't think he *wanted* to hurt anyone, yet these images tormented him.

My heart was so deeply moved by his desperation and that he would trust me with his story. I knew what was happening. He was being tormented and it wasn't okay! Nothing quite gets me fired up like this.

I expressed compassion and affirmed that he wasn't crazy. I described to him the demonic torment I was seeing. The moment I said those words, his face contorted and his muscles started bulging. He lunged toward me and hissed, "I hate you!"

I would be lying if I denied feeling a flash of fear, but just as quickly I remembered how much Jesus loves Reg and that I had the authority of Jesus for exactly such a moment. I calmly said, "Reg loves me and Jesus loves Reg. I bind you and gag you in the name of Jesus and command you to be silent and loosen your hold on Reg right now."

Reg immediately sat down with a huge gasp of breath. He stared at me wide-eyed and said, "What the eff just happened?!?"

I couldn't contain my joy! With a burst of laughter and great affection for my dear friend, I told him that Jesus had just set him free. I told him that those horrible thoughts had never been his, that they had been a type of torment sent to keep him bound in fear and shame.

He was a little embarrassed at how he had lashed out at me, but I reassured him that I had known it wasn't him. He was also in awe at the sense of clarity he was now experiencing. He no longer had any doubt about his sanity. That thing was not him and it was gone.

Reg has no shame telling this story. In fact, he stood up in front of the church and told everyone that he'd had an exorcism with me. Yes, a gasp went through the room, but he just laughed.

News this good needs to be shared. After all, men and women all around us are dying on the inside, so afraid that maybe they too are losing their minds.

Honestly, I live for these moments, even though it's not something I write on my business card. If you've engaged with the processes I have laid out, the enemy of your soul has already lost so much ground. His voice has lost influence. As you've experienced the loving presence of the Trinity, his lies have become so much more obvious and difficult to believe.

Yet you might still be experiencing torment and I don't want to leave you hanging, thinking that you don't have hope if everything you've tried so far has failed to help.

There's hope. So much hope.

I cannot emphasize enough how important it is to do the groundwork of the previous chapters. There are no shortcuts. But if you're still experiencing signs of torment, it's worth considering that you might be oppressed by a demonic entity.

Common signs of demonic torment are addiction that hasn't responded to usually successful treatments, an uncontrollable temper, sexual perversion (fantasized or acted out), compulsive behaviours, suicidal thoughts, self-harm, out-of-control thoughts, regular nightmares, recurrent flashes of unwanted images, and paranoia. Sometimes demonic torment manifests as physical pain that cannot be explained medically. Sometimes a demon presents as an imaginary friend. At best, these symptoms have an isolating effect on people, as they bind them in shame and confusion. At worst, they are absolutely destructive to the tormented individual and all their relationships.

The demonic gains a stronghold in our lives through traumatic events, our own willful participation in sinful activities, unforgiveness, occult practices, vows, curses, and sometimes even through family heritage. These are like open doors that we can close. They are grounds for the enemy to gain traction in our lives, but they can all be addressed. In fact, many of them have been already. Understanding how a demonic spirit is able to access us can help us to deal with the problem and close the door.

Of course, my friend Reg wondered how on earth this torment had come to be in his life. I briefly interviewed him along the lines of the contents of the previous chapters, but nothing obvious came up.

So we asked Jesus! We simply prayed, "Jesus, show us where this came into Reg's life."

He didn't have to think hard. A memory came to mind right away that seemed insignificant to him. When he was a young boy, he had been playing on the floor of his living room, as any little boy would. One of his relatives came into the room and sat on the floor beside him. After chatting a bit, the relative started tracing shapes on Reg's back and saying some words that Reg couldn't remember—but it definitely left him with some "creepy feelings."

Reg didn't know a lot about this relative, but he did know that the individual had been part of a secret society which had a practice of making vows (essentially curses) about themselves and the generations of their family.

I led Reg through forgiving his relative for doing this and praying a blessing over him. We also declared that Reg was free of the force and effect of these words because Jesus had taken all those curses upon Himself so Reg could be free (Galatians 3:13).

Remember my story at the beginning of the book about visiting my grandparents in the mental hospital? I spoke of a kind of darkness that crawled over me and landed in my tummy. That was a demonic presence. It was something I constantly had to fight off, contain, and manage. It was always there, siphoning off energy. And the only grounds it had to be there was generational familiarity.

One day I met a woman whom I could sense had the same gift I did to see and feel things in the spiritual atmosphere.

"You can see that I can see?" she replied when I asked her about it.

"Yes. I can see that you can see, and I want to know what you see."

What a ridiculous conversation! However, it led me to recognize this darkness as something other than just my own thoughts and feelings. I was then able to take authority over it in the name of Jesus and command it to leave. What an amazing day!

The enemy of your soul is a jerk and thinks nothing of exploiting the innocence of a child or the unmet needs of an adult. His purpose is destruction. I believe he's envious of the glory you are designed to carry. He banks on you resisting the love, grace, and authority of Jesus. Jesus has authority over the enemy and invites us to participate with Him in taking back territory that has been stolen. Jesus took all the sins you have committed, and all those done against you—every curse and every evil practice—so you could live free.

Across time and cultures, blood oaths and covenants have been considered the highest form of covenant bond. When Jesus died on the cross, He wrote a covenant in His own blood for your freedom. It is eternal and unbreakable (Hebrews 10:20). There is no greater expression of love than this ultimate sacrifice.

Jesus is all-in for your freedom. He invites you to join Him in this covenant.

THE TOOL

No amount of demonic torment can stand up to the authority of the name of Jesus. Before Jesus left the earth, He said that those who believe the good news of His freedom-bringing love would be able to drive out demons in the authority and power of His name (Mark 16:17).

The name of Jesus is the starting place of all deliverance from torment. Remember my story of being very afraid at night when I was six years old and calling on the name of Jesus? Fear left. Peace came. The name of Jesus is kryptonite to the enemy of your soul.

The name of Jesus is not to be used like some sort of magical formula, though. Jesus is the name of someone beloved and dear, the one who healed my broken heart and restored my fractured mind. It's no exclamation to be bandied about as a curse. It is truly powerful.

Simply saying the name of Jesus literally does make darkness flee. Say it like the treasure it is. It's the name of One who loved you so much that He put everything on the line for you.

Jesus. Say it in the dark. Say it when you're overwhelmed. Say it like a battle cry. Whisper it with sacred awe. Say the name of Jesus and darkness will flee.

The simple starting place is to speak the name of Jesus.

God always sends His Spirit when we call (Luke 11:13). If you sense the purpose and assignment of the torment inside you, such as fear, you can command it specifically:

In the name of Jesus, I command the spirit of fear/shame/seduction/control, etc. to leave me now. Go to Jesus and He will deal with you. Holy Spirit of God, please come and fill me now.

A full teaching and explanation of deliverance is beyond the scope of this book. You may need the help of someone with more experience to lead you through a more thorough process, but this is a good starting place.

You can find more resources listed at the back of this book if you think this is something you should pursue.

HERE'S HOPE

Many people get angsty and unsettled at the thought of demonic torment, but this is just one more strategy of the enemy to destroy your peace.

God brought you to this book. He has more goodness in store for you. If more deliverance is needed in your life, He is going to lead you to the resources you need. Praise Him and trust Him with the process.

WHAT'S IN A NAME?

Interlude

ABOUT A THOUSAND YEARS BEFORE JESUS WALKED THE FACE OF THE earth, one of His ancestors, King Solomon, wrote the words, *"The name of the Lord is a strong tower"* (Proverbs 18:10, KJV). I grew up singing songs based on this passage and honestly thought it made no sense at all. How on earth is a name a tower?

Fast-forward to adulthood and three children running around.

It seems my son came out of the womb hardwired to know exactly what would torment his sisters, especially the one directly next to him in birth order. Before he could crawl, he would reach out and yank her special blanket, eliciting shrieks of frustration from her and delight from him.

As they got older, he continued to hone his tormenting skills. I was often at my wits' end! None of my deterrents seemed to outweigh the irresistible delight of harassing her.

One day while working in the yard, I heard my daughter's cry of frustration and my son's joyful shout. He was chasing her and saying something I couldn't quite hear. She sounded like she was on her very last nerve.

"Mom!" she called when she saw me in the garden.

The minute my son heard her cry and saw me, he turned and ran in the other direction. While she was powerless to stop him, he knew I would stop him in no uncertain terms. It wouldn't end well for him.

I had a flash of understanding. I got it. The proverb was unpacked right before my eyes.

My daughter had no power or authority to stop him on her own, or she would have. The moment she called on my name, she invoked all the power and authority I carry. He knew that authority and had encountered the full force of it. There was no point in carrying on.

The enemy of our souls knows we have little power on our own. He knows Jesus loves us deeply. The moment we call on His name, we access a power and authority much greater than our own. He will come through for us.

Keep calling out the beautiful name of Jesus. His heart is tuned to your cry.

Love Without Coercion

Chapter Twenty-One

Taste and see…

—Psalm 34:8

THE ENEMY OF OUR SOULS IS CONSTANTLY TRYING TO SOW SEEDS OF discontent and rebellion in our hearts, hissing the lie that God's holding out on us. My heart breaks when I encounter people who bitterly think God is a cosmic, fun-wrecking bully who demands fidelity.

This book is my heart cry that you would discover the truth of His wild and extravagant love for you. He is like the kindest, fiercest Father you could ever imagine. He is fierce in wanting to protect you; His "rules" are meant to keep you safe from the deceitful and destructive ways of the enemy. He is fierce in how He fights for your restoration. He is so tender and kind in the way He has His arms wide open for you to run to Him when you mess up.

Being God and all, you would think He would command our trust, but He doesn't. Do you remember when I said that Jesus is the most perfect expression of who God is? Not once in any of the firsthand accounts of His life do we have a record of Him commanding trust or demanding allegiance. He challenges evil and calls out arrogance. He's fierce about injustice and oppression. To the broken and longing, He is gentle. He offers love without coercion.

Listen to His invitation:

Are you tired? Worn out? Burned out on religion? Come to me. Get away with me and you'll recover your life. I'll show you how

*to take a real rest. Walk with me and work with me—watch how
I do it. Learn the unforced rhythms of grace. I won't lay anything
heavy or ill-fitting on you. Keep company with me and you'll learn
to live freely and lightly.*

—Matthew 11:28–30, MSG

Read it again, slowly. Savour each phrase. It's irresistible in its
sweetness.

Come.

Recover.

Rest.

Unforced rhythms.

Freely and lightly.

Let your whole being sigh into the comfort and wholeness offered in
those words.

It is a wonder to me that Jesus offers healing and wholeness with no
strings attached. He simply offers and invites and, yet again, just like in
the original paradise, leaves us with a choice. You can go on your way or
you can follow Him.

There was a day when ten desperate men stood at a distance from
Jesus, crying out at the top of their lungs for mercy. They had a foul and
contagious skin disease that kept them isolated from society, their only
company others who were equally miserable and desperate. Jesus paused
what He was doing and told them to go see the priests who were the
guardians of public health at that time. As they obeyed His instructions,
they were healed.

One stopped when he realized what had happened and ran back to
Jesus to thank Him. The other nine went on their way, healed. No obligation. They were simply loved and restored, free to come or go.

Then there was Mary of Magdala, a woman tormented by seven demons. Tradition holds that she was a promiscuous woman, but there is no
record of this in scripture. I do know that the level of torment she experienced is usually the result of severe physical, emotional, or psychological

trauma. She would have felt helpless and hopeless, forever self-sabotaging, like a pawn in the hands of a sadist.

Until she met Jesus, who loves deeply and is all-in for restoration. He drove those demons out of her. Peace. Quiet. No more chaos or havoc. This is who He is and this is what He does.

Mary, too, was all-in after this, wildly in love—not in the erotic sense, but in the sense that there was no life for her apart from Him. There was nothing she wouldn't do for Jesus. She used her personal resources to support Jesus as He went about the country teaching and healing. There was nowhere she wouldn't go for love of Him, even to the cross. She was there when He was tortured to death, to the very last breath. And she was there at the crack of dawn to discover the empty tomb, feeling bewildered but perhaps also unsurprised because she had already tasted the power of resurrection. How could death hold the one who had brought her from death to life?

Her devotion left a mark. She is mentioned more than any other woman in the Gospels and more than most of the disciples.

Yet another man came to Jesus, attracted to the goodness in Him. This man was rich and had always tried to do the right thing. He wanted to know what it would take to access the fullness of life Jesus gives. When he found out that it would cost him everything, he was sad and went away. He was satisfied and content with what he had, so why would he risk it all on the possibility of something uncertain and perhaps difficult?

There is a cost to following Jesus, though it's not exactly an exchange in the traditional sense of the word. Because of love, you have been freely given the gift of your restoration.

Yet there's more. You can become part of the restoration story. You are invited to live the Jesus way of saying no to bitterness, anger, selfishness, pride, hiding, and self-gratification. These things are all part of the kingdom of darkness that harmed you in the first place.

Yet none of us can resist these things on our own strength. It's not a simple matter of stopping. Rather, we have to yield and say yes. Followers of Jesus aren't just people who try really hard to stop doing bad things and start doing good things. They've encountered a radical love that displaces darkness. They live freely and powerfully out of that love.

Jesus was a terrible salesman. He didn't candy-coat the call to those who wanted to follow Him. He said,

> *If any of you wants to be my follower, you must give up your own way, take up your cross daily, and follow me. If you try to hang on to your life, you will lose it. But if you give up your life for my sake, you will save it. And what do you benefit if you gain the whole world but are yourself lost or destroyed?*
>
> —Luke 9:23–25

It wouldn't be easy, but worth it.

When He lived and walked on the earth, Jesus healed every kind of disease and torment. He brought outcasts back into community. He called out injustice. There was no limit to what He could restore. He was captivating and disruptive. His goodness was winsome and convicting. People either loved Him or hated Him, but encountering Him always elicited a response.

You have encountered Jesus in these pages. Picture Him sitting across from you right now, a bit of a smile teasing around His lips and one eyebrow slightly raised. What is your response?

He's no dictator who demands our fidelity. He invites us and is unflinching in acknowledging that following Him will cost you. He also promises that it will be worth it. But you get to pick.

He's hoping you are all-in, because He has an adventure in store for you!

If you're still not sure, He will wait. His love is radical like that.

THE TOOL

Choosing to take up your cross daily is a simple act of your will.

I have prayed the following Lordship prayer almost every day for many years. To declare Jesus is Lord of your life is to say that you are choosing Him, His authority, and His influence over you. The following declarations are a fresh reminder of the choice I have made and all the ways it applies to the small moments of my day. It has often helped me not to take the bait of the enemy. Simply pray:

Jesus, I admit that I want my own way, but I choose You. Thank You for saving, healing, and restoring me. Today I choose to walk in step with You. I invite You to be Lord of every area of my life.

Lord of my relationship with you and my relationships with others.

Lord of my thoughts, dreams, and desires.

Lord of my emotions and my reactions.

Lord of all my choices and decisions.

Lord of my body, my health, my eating, my exercise, my rest, and my appearance.

Lord of my entertainment, what I look at and listen to.

Lord of my mouth and what I say.

Lord of my work.

Lord of my sexuality.

Lord of my resources, time, finances, and energy.

Lord of my marriage and parenting.

Lord of my perceived needs.

Jesus, I long for more freedom for myself and the world around me. Please teach me how to walk in a new way. I want to know You more and more. I want to show others how wonderful You are. Thank You for Your limitless grace. Amen.

HERE'S HOPE

Surrendering the right to live our own way isn't easy. It's often downright uncomfortable.

And it is totally worth it. In the same way you have experienced brokenness and harmed others through your brokenness, you can live in the way of restoration and bring more restoration to the world around you.

The more you surrender to the Jesus way, the more you experience His joy and goodness. This enables you to love others well, which allows them, too, to get a taste of restoration. You become an encounter with Jesus. It gets addictive.

NOW
WHAT?

Chapter Twenty-Two

As one goes forward in time, the net entropy (degree of disorder) of any isolated or closed system will always increase (or at least stay the same).[22]

—The Second Law of Thermodynamics

IN TALKING ABOUT THE PROCESS LAID OUT IN THIS BOOK, I'VE LOST count of the number of people who've told me they tried something like this once before, but it didn't work. I sigh. Perhaps too forcefully. It's easier to live in freedom than bondage, but it's also easier to keep doing what you've always done than to develop new habits. That takes deliberate effort. Alertness.

Abraham Lincoln is credited with saying that most people are as happy as they make up their minds to be, and I think there's a lot of truth in that. Thankful people are far and away happier than complainers. Yet we cannot simply think our way into spiritual health. We will always run into a dead end if we fail to consider the spiritual dimension. The spiritual dimension affects the mind and vice versa. Thus, this book.

I have worked with many people who have gone to counselling for years but felt like they stalled. When they recognized that there was a spiritual dimension to their struggle and learned how to address that, they catapulted into health because all the years of counselling had established wonderful scaffolding in their souls. With the spiritual blockages removed, they were in good shape to move forward and flourish.

Others have very little framework for emotional health. That's okay, too. They're simply starting the journey in a different place. For them, dealing with spiritual strongholds made it so much easier to begin establishing healthy thoughts and emotions.

We simply cannot overlook the need to deal with spiritual strongholds. In order to continue walking forward in health and freedom, I recommend various resources. Some of these are listed at the back of this book. You will discover others as you ask God to continue to guide you on this pathway.

There are no quick fixes. There are wonderful moments of encounter that set us on a new trajectory. Remember, God isn't your fairy godmother. He does, however, set us on a new path. He brought you to this space and time. As you move forward in new ways, you will end up in a vastly different place.

Perhaps you've heard the analogy of a flight leaving New York with a one-degree error in its course to Los Angles. That flight won't make it to Los Angeles; it will land many miles out in the ocean. A small step in a new direction today, sustained over time, will land you in a vastly different place than your original course.

Each person who encounters this book will have a different story and a unique path. However, there are four things I consider essential if you're going to move forward with this new trajectory. They are simple, but not always easy. Failing to engage in the deliberate steps of walking forward in freedom will result in entropy—a general decline into disorder.

BOSS OF YOUR THOUGHTS

Think about what you're thinking about. The great reformer Martin Luther compared thoughts to birds and said, "You cannot keep birds from flying over your head but you can keep them from building a nest in your hair."[23]

These words are profoundly true! The thoughts that flit through our minds are a confluence of many things—our upbringing, habits, experiences, biology (hunger, hormones, sleep deprivation, etc.), and of course the unseen spiritual dimension.

Now What?

In his letter to the Ephesians, the Apostle Paul describes the assault of the enemy of our souls as *"fiery arrows"* (Ephesians 6:16). This resonates with me! Some days it feels relentless.

Yet we are not the victim of these thoughts. We don't have to embrace them. However, plenty of our thought patterns have been solidified long before we knew what was happening. They can feel so normal that we don't even recognize them as a problem.

You've had millions of experiences in your lifetime. Each experience has triggered emotions and you've developed thoughts around those experiences. Those thoughts literally become matter in your brain. Repeated thoughts build circuits that become pathways.

Your brain has trillions of these neural connections. These circuits look like trees in your brain. When you break agreement with a deeply rooted thought pattern, picture yourself digging up a tree by the roots or taking an axe to the root. The beauty of the breaking agreement tool is that you don't just get rid of a thought, you plant a new one. What does Jesus have for you in place of the old way of thinking? That which He gives you is like the seed of a new tree. You need to plant it, water it, and weed it until it becomes established as your new normal.

I cannot emphasize enough the importance of developing new habits of thought. I was two years into my healing journey when I had the wonderful realization that my struggle with depression was over. I was free! The underlying wounds were healed and I had developed new ways of thinking that alerted me to seeds of depression before they could take root.

However, you don't have to wait two whole years for significant change! It only takes twenty-one days of reinforcing a new thought habit for protein changes to happen and create long-term memory in your brain.[24] Your healing will solidify as you take charge of your thoughts, quickly identifying old habits and building new ones.

You need to keep the breaking agreement tool in your pocket until it's a deeply ingrained habit. I continue to use it daily. Just this morning, I awoke with a sense of heaviness that I knew was connected to a conflict I had yesterday. I couldn't shake it, so I asked Jesus what it was. It turned out I was feeling hopeless. So I broke agreement with hopelessness and the heaviness lifted. I was able to get out of bed and start my day with energy and joy.

We aren't victims of all our thoughts and feelings. Neither are we fully able to sort them out on our own. Check in with the Architect of your restoration regularly.

ACTS OF WAR

Make deliberate choices to walk in a new way. Whatever it is you're trying to overcome, there is an opposite behaviour you can practice intentionally.

I used to be so hypersensitive to any sort of criticism or feedback. I was protecting my wounds, but this defence mechanism also kept me from recognizing areas in which my natural habits and predispositions kept me from flourishing.

So I learned a powerful new response: "Thank you for sharing that with me. I'll think about it."

Let me tell you, this really threw a curveball into our marital arguments! There's no power struggle in that phrase, just a willingness to take responsibility. Instead of shutting down in my workplace or throwing up my shield, this phrase has helped me grow and remain engaged.

There have definitely been times when I had to process things that weren't said in a good spirit, or maybe they were even said outright unkindly, but I took them and sorted through the rubble. I found comfort for the discomfort in the presence of Jesus, broke agreement with all the old lies that wanted to sneak in through the pain, and began to walk in a new way.

New actions paired with a healed heart are incredibly catalytic. Ask Jesus how He wants to lead you in acts of war against your old ways of living.

COMMUNITY

One of the most critical things you can do in setting this new trajectory is to find a community that's also on a journey of spiritual and emotional wholeness. There actually are churches like that out there! There are groups of people who seek authentic community as a place of support, encouragement, and growth.

The trick to this, of course, is that most of our greatest pain has come from human interactions. It's sometimes hard for us to believe that it isn't good to be alone. Alone feels safe, and being in community pretty much guarantees that broken places will collide. There will be risk and sometimes discomfort in community.

Yet there will be healing also, healing that cannot come any other way. On the days when I can't remember who I am and what's true about me, I need someone who can look me straight in the eyes and tell me what is true. On days when I've blown it, I need to confess my brokenness to another person as an act of war on shame and see grace in the eyes of another. I also need them to challenge and encourage me to take the next steps.

Perhaps this idea triggers thoughts of exactly why you know you should not or cannot be in community. This is an invitation to look at that pain from your past. Is there someone you need to forgive? Perhaps several people! What agreements have you made about community, the church, and people? What judgments have you made? You may need to break some soul ties. We've all had negative experiences in community, but that's just the assault of the enemy against the goodness God has planned for us in His design that we are better together.

Ask Jesus to lead you to a growing community of believers. You don't just need them—they need you! Seek out this group with the understanding that you'll be growing in that community and becoming that community at the same time. It won't work out well if you go in with the idea that the rest of the community needs to meet your needs and have it all together. I've seen this parasitic expectation take people out more times than I can count. A healthy community is symbiotic. There is a give and take. You are neither victim nor saviour, rather an essential part of a complex organism.

You will have days when you want to turtle and days when you want to lash out. This is simply a dashboard indicator of an opportunity for healing and growth. Instead, tuck yourself away. Jesus did. There were times when He withdrew from the crowds to have an encounter with His

Father. Take time to do the same. Use these tools. Read the Bible. You will be strengthened and ready to lean in again.

INSPIRED INSTRUCTION

About the Bible—read it. It's full of truth and tells of Jesus, who is truth personified. So much of my self-defeating thinking has been revealed for what it is because I've positioned myself to encounter Jesus through the regular reading of scriptures. The more we look at Him, the more we are changed into His beautiful likeness (2 Corinthians 3:16–18).

Your soul has habits just like your body and mind. It will take time to build new patterns, but it's worth it. Don't let discouragement take you out. Simply recognize that you're breaking an old pattern and move on. Maintain a sense of humour! Laugh at yourself. Laugh at the enemy. Breathe in fresh joy and hope and get moving onward and upward.

In order for true life transformation to take place, you'll need to re-visit the tools in this book many times. In some ways, the journey never ends, but it becomes easier as you develop new habits and make a practice of seeing things in a new way. Your friendship with Jesus will continually deepen as you walk in step with Him. Your healing and restoration are contagious—as you walk in these new ways, you're going to become a catalyst for healing in the lives around you. He has so many adventures in store for you!

THE TOOL

Remember the three people who encountered Jesus in the previous chap-ter? His healing and love were freely given. Their response was theirs to give. What they chose made all the difference in the trajectory of their lives.

The tools are yours to develop now with the help of the great Ar-chitect of your restoration. Ask Jesus to lead you in action steps based on this chapter.

What thoughts need to be nipped in the bud? What acts of war do you need to execute? Who do you need to reach out to in order to form community? How can you integrate Scripture reading into your lifestyle?

HERE'S HOPE

We read in 1 Thessalonians 5:24, *"The one who calls you by name is trustworthy and will thoroughly complete his work in you"* (TPT). This is really good news. You want to be alert, but you don't need to be anxious or strive. This is the journey of a lifetime, not a to-do list. Keep your feet on the right path and you'll get where you want to go. Enjoy the ride!

YOU ARE DANGEROUS

Chapter Twenty-Three

But the lovers of God walk on the highway of light, and their way shines brighter and brighter until the perfect day.

—Proverbs 4:18, TPT

MY FAMILY HAS A FAVOURITE PLACE TO CAMP AT A LITTLE LAKE TUCKED away in northern British Columbia. Until a few years ago, there was no cell service there, which made it a perfect getaway. Sunshine, water, good books, and campfires are my perfect recipe for rejuvenation.

I usually bring something to read aloud around the fire. Two years ago, I was reading aloud Donald Miller's excellent book *Scary Close* when I came upon a question with a blank to be filled: "I only matter if _____."[25] I didn't even need to pause. Without hesitation, I said, "I only matter if I make people happy."

Boom.

What?

Seriously?

Remember when I told you about the season of great sadness? During that period, I learned that people will be sad and I am loved and cherished when I make them feel better.

I've been doing this healthy soul work for years. I help other people with it daily. Yet this subtle lie still had traction. There was no question that this was a rank lie and that on some level I believed it. A speedbump in my soul.

What an unpleasant surprise... and what a sweet gift to know that I could live free of its sneaky weight.

I tell you this to encourage you on your restoration journey. It is a journey, not a destination. Keep going! Live expectant that the great Architect of your restoration will continue to lead you on the way that shines brighter and brighter. Stay humble. Keep learning.

New seasons and new challenges have a way of stirring up old feelings and habits. Whenever I find myself there again, I celebrate the fact that though I might be going around the same mountain again, I'm further up the mountain and the journey is getting shorter and taking me higher. Don't let discouragement stop you in your tracks. Keep going!

Remember to be kind to yourself and others. When we do this deep work of removing boulders and barriers, it's like the furniture has been moved from where it has always been. It's inevitable that you and the people around you will trip over this newly relocated furniture. Make sure you keep laughing and celebrate the fact that this new way is so much better even if it's a little awkward at first.

You are dangerous. There's no neutral Switzerland when it comes to those unseen players on the stage of your story. There's darkness and light, and it's one or the other. When you buy the lie of neutrality, you are actually giving way to the darkness.

How is that, you ask? Because when you live boldly and bravely loved, you're so dangerous to the enemy who wants to destroy all the creative, flourishing glory of your destiny.

You matter. When you show up, stuff happens. When you retreat, shut down, and play it safe, you're no longer a threat to the darkness. You're always picking one and being dangerous to the other. Be fierce and be dangerous against the darkness.

Perhaps you feel tremors of regret. Because of those years when you didn't know, when you willingly and recklessly partnered with the darkness, you may feel empty-handed and aware of the fact that you've taken others down with you along the way. Regret can be debilitating. Jesus has His arms wide open in invitation, offering to help you take it from here. And then some.

I leave you with this parting dose of hope: you get double restoration for everything you've lost along the way.

Because of the covenant I made with you, sealed with blood, I will free your prisoners from death in a waterless dungeon. Come back to the place of safety, all you prisoners who still have hope! I promise this very day that I will repay two blessings for each of your troubles.
—Zechariah 9:11–12

I love that promise! The best kind of revenge on the enemy of your soul is to run to that place of safety, lay hold of your promise, and take back double the land you've lost. Break agreement with shame and regret.

What does Jesus have for you instead? For sure He has more love for you and those who've been harmed in your story. Restoration. Hope. He also has adventures for you. They will be risky and pull you out of your comfort zone, but you will never feel more alive or satisfied than when you're living your purpose freely and fully.

I am living proof. I was once so full of anxiety and self-consciousness, secretly bleeding hopelessness and death. One day at a time, Jesus met me and restored the broken places, closed up the haemorrhaging wounds, purged the infection, and strengthened me through fresh encounters with His love. He lit a fire inside me, a fierce desire that no one else would suffer without hope either.

Then one day He beckoned me to put on red shoes as a symbol of my willingness to be seen and known. I was so afraid. Again, this was new territory. But it was worth the risk because you, dear reader, needed to hear this message.

Your restoration and freedom are not just for you. You are meant to be a beacon of hope to a world that's starving for hope. Everyone needs an introduction to the real Jesus. He's not just a far-off deity. Everyone needs an encounter with His healing love. Be contagious with hope. Be fiercely hopeful. The world is hungry for it, just waiting for you to show up.

Be loved.

Be free.

Be dangerous.

THE
TOOLS

As promised, here is the framework of tools I have unpacked throughout
the book. These aren't magic formulas. Rather, they are principles that
will lead you to and help you maintain spiritual and emotional health in
conjunction with other good practices.

FEELING WORDS

Irritated	Furious	Adventurous
Disappointed	Guilty	Tender
Discouraged	Abandoned	Optimistic
Afraid	Bitter	Energized
Annoyed	Hateful	Calm
Ashamed	Heavy-hearted	Joyful
Hopeless	Vulnerable	Excited
Anxious	Betrayed	Peaceful
Offended	Frustrated	Grateful
Unworthy	Crushed	Free
Powerless	Distressed	Content
Confused	Useless	Powerful
Angry	Hopeful	Bold
Unloved	Curious	Cherished
Alone	Loving	
Suspicious	Delighted	

BREAKING AGREEMENT

In the name of Jesus, I break every agreement I have made with
_____. I command _____ out of my thoughts and
emotions, out of my actions and reactions, away from how I see
myself and others, and away from my marriage and my children (if applicable). Jesus, I ask that You take this far away from
me. What do You have for me instead?

FORGIVENESS

Thank You, God, for Your love. As an act of my will, I choose to
forgive (offender) for (name their actions). This made me feel
(name the cost and feelings: afraid, unable to trust, abandoned,
ashamed, insignificant, hopeless, rejected, etc.). It caused (name
any fallout in your life). I give all of this pain and loss to You,
Jesus, and I put all my hope in You to restore everything that
has been lost and broken. I now release (offender) from any obligation to make things right with me and I release them from
the judgments I have made. I bless them with (knowing they
are deeply loved, etc.).

AUTHORITY OVER DEMONIC PRESENCE

In the name of Jesus, I command the spirit of fear/shame/se-
duction/control, etc. to leave me now. Go to Jesus and He will
deal with you. Holy Spirit of God, please come and fill me now.

BREAKING SOUL TIES

For a relationship that is *over*, pray the following out loud:

I place the cross of Jesus Christ between me and _____.

In the name of Jesus, I break all ties formed between us. (If the relationship was physical, break all "spirit, soul, and body ties.")

In the name of Jesus, I send back to _____ all parts of themself that they gave to me. In the name of Jesus, I take back from _____ all parts of myself that I gave to them.

Holy Spirit of God, please set a watch over my soul to keep me from forming any unhealthy ties with them again.

For a relationship that is *ongoing*, pray the following out loud:

I place the cross of Jesus Christ between me and _____. In the name of Jesus, I break any and all unhealthy ties formed between us.

In the name of Jesus, I send back to _____ all parts of themself that they gave to me outside of God's design.

In the name of Jesus, I take back from _____ all parts of myself that I gave to them outside God's design.

I bless and I keep the relationship God has for us.

Holy Spirit of God, please set a watch over my soul to keep me from forming any unhealthy ties with them again.

Breathe deeply. Release the other person. Receive wholeness for yourself. Ask Jesus if there is anything He wants you to know about this relationship.

LORDSHIP PRAYER

Jesus, I admit that I want my own way, but I choose You. Thank You for saving, healing, and restoring me. Today I choose to walk in step with You. I invite You to be Lord of every area of my life.

Lord of my relationship with you and my relationships with others.

Lord of my thoughts, dreams, and desires.

Lord of my emotions and my reactions.

Lord of all my choices and decisions.

Lord of my body, my health, my eating, my exercise, my rest, and my appearance.

Lord of my entertainment, what I look at and listen to.

Lord of my mouth and what I say.

Lord of my work.

Lord of my sexuality.

Lord of my resources, time, finances, and energy.

Lord of my marriage and parenting.

Lord of my perceived needs.

Jesus, I long for more freedom for myself and the world around me. Please teach me how to walk in a new way. I want to know You more and more. I want to show others how wonderful You are. Thank You for Your limitless grace. Amen.

POUR OUT YOUR HEART TO GOD

Healthy Lament:

O my people, trust in him at all times. Pour out your heart to him, for God is our refuge.

—Psalms 62:8

Begin by considering these questions.

What sadness, frustration, or disappointment is He inviting you to bring to Him? If something seemingly random comes up, go with it! Jesus knows things we don't.

How does this situation make you feel? This is the time to be brutally honest with God. He can handle it. We do ourselves no favours when we minimize our pain, both to ourselves and to God, to make it more "appropriate."

Ask Jesus if there's anyone You need to forgive or break ties with. It may be yourself or God. Use the following tools, adapting them to your situation:

Thank You, Jesus, for forgiving me. I forgive (offender) for (specific action). It made me feel _____. I release (offender) of any obligation to make things right with me. I place all of this on You, Jesus, and put all my hope in You to restore all things. I release (offender) of judgments I have made. I bless (offender) with _____.

In the name of Jesus and by the power of the cross, I break all ungodly body, soul, and spirit ties formed between me and _____. I send back to _____ all parts of them that they gave me outside of God's design and take back what I gave of myself to them outside of God's design. I bless and keep the relationship You have for us. I ask You, Jesus, to set a guard that I may never again connect with _____ in this way. As I break this soul tie, what is the truth about this situation You want me to know?

Break agreement with anything that isn't truth from Jesus. Pay attention to repeated phrases that could indicate agreement:

In the name of Jesus and by the power of the cross, I break every agreement I have made, known or unknown, with _____. I repent of joining with these things. I take authority over _____ and command it out of my thoughts and my emotions, out of my actions and reactions, away from how I see myself and others, away from my marriage and my children (if applicable), and completely out of my destiny and calling! _____, go to Jesus now. Jesus, what do You have for me instead?

Ask God or Jesus to show you His presence in the memory or in the moment.
Remember God's promises about your situation.
Ask Him if He has any action steps for you to take.
Ask Him to teach you how to walk in a new way.
Then anchor all of this in worship, praise, and thanksgiving.

RECOMMENDED RESOURCES

Here are just a few favourite books that have challenged and cheered my journey:

Desmond Tutu and Mpho Tutu, *The Book of Forgiving: The Fourfold Path for Healing Ourselves and Our World* (San Francisco, CA: Harper One, 2014).

David G. Benner, *The Gift of Being Yourself* (Downers Grove, IL: Inter-Varsity Press, 2015).

Dr. Randy Clark, *Biblical Guidebook to Deliverance* (Lake Mary, FL: Charisma House, 2015).

Blake K. Healy, *Indestructible* (Lake Mary, FL: Charisma House, 202)0.

Donald Miller, *Scary Close* (Nashville, TN: Thomas Nelson, 2015).

Dr. Rob Reimer, *Soul Care* (Franklin, TN: Carpenter's Son Publisher, 2016).

Dr. Caroline Leaf, *Switch on Your Brain* (Grand Rapids, MI: Baker Books, 2015).

Also, check out the podcast I host with Amy Cheetham, *Further Up and Further In*. We release biweekly episodes to encourage you in your journey.

ACKNOWLEDGEMENTS

There's no way for me to adequately thank all the beautiful people who journey with me in life. This book is the fulfillment of words spoken decades ago and prayers prayed by many over the years. There are a few who must be specifically named, and even then it is a long list. I am humbled by the kindness and generosity of so many!

My beta readers. Every subsequent reader is blessed because of you! Your gift of time and honest feedback was priceless. You made this book so much better. I pray that you will continue to be blessed with ever-increasing hope in your own lives. Farrell, Amy, Joy, Colin, Rebekah, Jon, Mickey, and Ken, thank you from the bottom of my heart!

My photographer friend. Remember years ago when I was off changing a diaper and you saw some of my writing left on the table? You said I should get it published and I shared my dream of a book. We've launched those babies since then and made many memories together. I'm thankful for all the ones you captured through your lens. Melanie, thanks for the great headshot for letting me see the world through your eyes.

My church family. Thank you for letting me practice on you and releasing me to this assignment. Being your pastor will always rank as one of the greatest privileges of my life. I don't feel worthy of all the love and prayers, but I am forever grateful. Beaverlodge Alliance Church, you truly are one of a kind.

My "support gang." You are always believing in me in ways that surprise, bewilder, and inspire me. I cannot imagine surviving the last year in all its strangeness of COVID, change in vocation, and the solitary journey of writing without you holding me and cheering me on. Dave, Rose, and Carrie, I suspect you're right—this is just the beginning. There will be books. Starleigh, Boyd, and Esther, I'm so glad you joined us and have been part of cheerfully but relentlessly pushing me across the finish line.

My gym family. Thanks for keeping me healthy and strong and cheering on this project. I was constantly amazed at your keen interest. Sweating out the writer's block was just what I needed some days. Nicknaming me Soulseeker was its own benediction. I love you guys! Lindsay and Konrad and the OT team, may you experience fierce hope.

The ministries that helped me through some of the hardest renovations. Readers will find in these pages variations on tools I have learned from many people. I have been specifically blessed through Nothing Hidden Ministries and Ellel Ministries. Through your obedience and the many volunteers who make your events happen, my life has been radically changed.

My ministry partner. I love the strength in our oppositeness. You've been along for much of the ride as this material became a broader ministry. Your insights have helped me frame it in ways that have made it relatable for more people, and podcasting with you is a blast. Amy, you love so well. Thank you.

My parents. You are my heroes in so many ways. You lived through the darkest parts of this story and showed me how to turn to Jesus. You couldn't change the trauma, but you gave me the most important key for finding hope in it all. This book and the lives it will touch are part of your legacy of faithfulness. I love you so much!

My husband. Thank you for hanging in there through the worst of the renovations. I cannot thank you enough for lending your rock-solid faith to the adventure of leaving the safety of my day job for this assignment. Your faith in God's call on me continues to make my eyes leak a little. The twinkle in your eyes every time you nudged me to admit I was writing a book made me brave. Let's have more adventures together!

My kids. I know you love to have the last word, so I'll give it to you here. For some reason, even though you've rolled your eyes at my words countless times, you definitely thought I should write a book. And then said I should write more in a "next one." You've checked in, cheered me on, and celebrated milestones. You continue to delight me and you'll always be my greatest legacy. Heather, Kaleigh, and Devin, I'd say something mushy, but you'd make gagging noises so I'll just say thanks for the grey hairs and the laugh lines. May you always live in fierce hope. Love you forever.

ABOUT
THE AUTHOR

Michelle Dwyer is a laughing, red-shoe-wearing dealer of hope. She is passionate about igniting fires of hope and equipping others to live in emotional and spiritual health so they can flourish and transform the world around them. She speaks at workshops, conferences and retreats, sometimes blogs, and regularly releases a podcast. All of this is fuelled by her desire for everyone to encounter the dynamic, loving presence of God who restored her broken heart and tormented mind. Her resume includes legal assistant, teacher, and pastor. She has almost completed an MA in Leadership and Ministry from Ambrose University and makes her home in Alberta with her husband Brian and their three mostly grownup kids. You can check out her website at www.michelledwyer.ca and her podcast, *Further Up and Further In,* can be found on most platforms.

ENDNOTES

1   "Sadness is but a wall…" *Quotes.net*. Date of access: September 7, 2021 (https://www.quotes.net/quote/2836).

2   Elie Wiesel, *Night* (New York, NY: Hill and Wang, 2006), 5. Translated from the French by Marion Wiesel.

3   "Lao Tzu," *BBC Learning English*. Date of access: September 7, 2021 (https://www.bbc.co.uk/worldservice/learningenglish/moving-words/shortlist/laotzu.shtml).

4   "Bono Talks Jesus with Focus On The Family's Jim Daley," *Huffington Post*. August 24, 2013 (https://www.huffpost.com/entry/bono-jesus-focus-on-the-family_n_3491753).

5   Bear in mind that this can be done in a way that implies a threat, which totally defeats the purpose.

6   Neuroscientist Dr. Caroline Leaf has done great work on this. I recommend her podcast, blog, and numerous books on the science around this subject.

7   "Myiasis," *Wikipedia*. Date of access: December 11, 2020 (https://en.wikipedia.org/wiki/Myiasis).

8   By the way, I think "fine" is just another four-letter word. We were created for so much more than fine!

9   David G. Benner, *The Gift of Being Yourself* (Downers Grove, IL: InterVarsity Press, 2015), 72.

10 "Lament," *Wikipedia*. Date of access: September 20, 2021 (https://en.wikipedia.org/wiki/Lament).

11 "Lament," *Urban Dictionary*. Date of access: August 30, 2021 (https://www.urbandictionary.com/define.php?term=lament).

12 C.S. Lewis, *The Complete C.S. Lewis* (New York, NY: HarperCollins, 2002), 98.

13 Desmond Tutu and Mpho Tutu, *The Book of Forgiving: The Fourfold Path for Healing Ourselves and Our World* (New York, NY: HarperCollins, 2014), 71.

14 Ibid., 60.

15 This tip has done wonders for keeping my marriage in a much healthier state.

16 Jon Tyson, *Beautiful Resistance: The Joy of Conviction in a Culture of Compromise* (Colorado Springs, CO: Mulnomah Press, 2020), 48.

17 Caroline Leaf, *The Perfect You* (Grand Rapids, MI: Baker Books, 2017), 56, 62.

18 Daniel J. Siegel, M.D., and Mary Hartzell, M.Ed., *Parenting from the Inside Out* (New York, NY: Tarcher Perigee, 2014), 108.

19 Melody Beattie, *Codependent No More* (Center City, MN: Hazelden Foundation, 1987), 31.

20 Dr. Rob Reimer, "There is no transformation..." *Facebook.* January 25, 2021 (https://www.facebook.com/DrRobReimer/posts/4216328068394027).

21 Steven M. Southwick and Dennis S. Charney, *Resilience: The Science of Mastering Life's Greatest Challenges* (Cambridge, UK: Cambridge University Press, 2018), 70.

22 "Entropy (arrow of time)," *Wikipedia.* Date of access: September 7, 2021 (https://en.wikipedia.org/wiki/Entropy_(arrow_of_time)).

23 "You cannot keep birds from flying..." *Quotepark.com.* Date of access: September 7, 2021 (https://quotepark.com/quotes/1329168-martin-luther-you-cannot-keep-birds-from-flying-over-your-head-b/).

24 Caroline Leaf, *Switch on Your Brain* (Grand Rapids: Baker Books, 2013), 128.

25 Donald Miller, *Scary Close* (Nashville, TN: Thomas Nelson, 2015), 21.